Routledge Revivals

Point of View

The purpose of *Point of View*, first published in 1990, is twofold: from the perspective of linguistics, to analyse the discourse structure of texts; from the perspective of literary studies, to explain certain non-linguistic aspects of the texts in terms of linguistic form. This study therefore aims to provide a balanced and comprehensive account of the relationship between linguistic form and point of view. It will be of particular value to literature students with an interest in linguistics and literary style.

Point of View
A Linguistic Analysis of Literary Style

Susan Ehrlich

First published in 1990
by Routledge

This edition first published in 2014 by Routledge
2 Park Square, Milton Park, Abingdon, Oxon, OX14 4RN
and by Routledge
711 Third Avenue, New York, NY 10017

Routledge is an imprint of the Taylor & Francis Group, an informa business

© 1990 Susan Ehrlich

The right of Susan Ehrlich to be identified as author of this work has been asserted by her in accordance with sections 77 and 78 of the Copyright, Designs and Patents Act 1988.

All rights reserved. No part of this book may be reprinted or reproduced or utilised in any form or by any electronic, mechanical, or other means, now known or hereafter invented, including photocopying and recording, or in any information storage or retrieval system, without permission in writing from the publishers.

Publisher's Note
The publisher has gone to great lengths to ensure the quality of this reprint but points out that some imperfections in the original copies may be apparent.

Disclaimer
The publisher has made every effort to trace copyright holders and welcomes correspondence from those they have been unable to contact.

A Library of Congress record exists under LC control number: 89049500

ISBN 13: 978-1-138-77947-1 (hbk)
ISBN 13: 978-1-315-77125-0 (ebk)
ISBN 13: 978-1-138-77953-2 (pbk)

POINT OF VIEW

A Linguistic Analysis of Literary Style

Susan Ehrlich

London and New York

First published 1990
by Routledge
11 New Fetter Lane, London EC4P 4EE

Simultaneously published in the USA and Canada
by Routledge
a division of Routledge, Chapman and Hall, Inc.
29 West 35th Street, New York, NY 10001

© 1990 Susan Ehrlich

Typeset by Selectmove Ltd, London
Printed in Great Britain by
Biddles Ltd, Guildford

All rights reserved. No part of this book may be reprinted or reproduced or utilized in any form or by any electronic, mechanical, or other means, now known or hereafter invented, including photocopying and recording, or in any information storage or retrieval system, without permission in writing from the publishers.

British Library Cataloguing in Publication Data
Ehrlich, Susan
Point of view: a linguistic analysis of literary style.
1. Literature. Style. Linguistic aspects
I. Title
808'.02
ISBN 0-415-04139-2

Library of Congress Cataloging in Publication Data
Ehrlich, Susan.
Point of view: a linguistic analysis of literary style / Susan Ehrlich.
p. cm.
Includes bibliographical references.
1. Point of view (Literature)   2. Discourse analysis, Literary.
3. Space and time in literature.   I. Title.
PN3383.P64E37   1990
401'.41—dc20
ISBN 0-415-04139-2 (U.S.)

TO THE MEMORY OF CARLOS YORIO

CONTENTS

Acknowledgements		vii
Abbreviations		ix
Introduction		1
1	SENTENCE-BASED APPROACHES TO POINT OF VIEW	4
	Introduction	4
	General description	6
	Limitations of sentence-based approaches to RST	17
	RST/narration and foreground/background	25
2	COHESION, COHERENCE, AND EPISODES	27
	Introduction	27
	Coherence	28
	Explicit coherence: cohesion	30
	Summary	39
3	REFERENTIAL AND SEMANTIC CONNECTOR LINKING	40
	Introduction	40
	Dominance and sentences containing parentheticals	41
	Cohesion and sentences containing parentheticals	48
	Demarcation of discourse units	56
	Summary	57

4	**TEMPORAL LINKING**	58
	Introduction	58
	Temporal linking as a cohesive device	59
	Interpretation of temporal expressions	60
	Temporal interpretation of sentences of RST	64
	Anchoring predicates	74
	Demarcation of discourse units	78
	Summary	80
5	**ASPECT, COHERENCE, AND POINT OF VIEW**	81
	Introduction	81
	Past progressive and point of view	83
	Progressive vs simple aspect	87
	Progressive in other contexts	92
	Conclusion	93
6	**CONCLUSIONS**	95
	Introduction	95
	Summary: cohesion, coherence, and RST	95
	Summary: demarcation of RST units	99
	Function of RST inter-sentential devices	101
7	**IMPLICATIONS: THE FOREGROUND/BACKGROUND DISTINCTION**	106
	Introduction	106
	The foreground/background distinction	106
	Narration/RST and foreground/background	110
	Linguistic correlates of foreground and background material	115
	Notes	118
	References	125
	Subject index	130
	Author index	132

ACKNOWLEDGEMENTS

This book is a substantially revised version of my 1986 University of Toronto PhD dissertation. In revising it for publication, I have reorganized Chapters 2 and 3, added substantial portions to Chapters 2, 3, 4, and 6, and included a new final chapter, Chapter 7: Implications: the foreground/background distinction.

Many friends and colleagues have contributed to the development of my thesis and this book. I am particularly indebted to Jack Chambers, for his careful attention to all aspects of my work and for his gentle prodding and encouragement during the ambivalent stages of my graduate school career. I thank members of my dissertation committee, Paul Hopper, Debbie James, Ivan Kalmar, Keren Rice, and Ron Wardhaugh, and two anonymous Routledge reviewers for valuable suggestions and advice concerning the revision of my dissertation manuscript. While not directly involved in the writing of my thesis or this book, Carlos Yorio contributed significantly to my intellectual development through his teaching and general enthusiastic encouragement of my work. I only regret that I can no longer thank Carlos in person.

In a less direct way, I am indebted to Ann Banfield, Helen Dry, and Tanya Reinhart. Their influence on the ideas presented in this book is profound and I can only apologize if I have managed to misrepresent their work in any way.

I am grateful to the Social Sciences and Humanities Research Council of Canada for doctoral fellowships during the writing of my dissertation and to the Faculty of Arts, York University, for a research grant that provided funding during the final stages of revision. I acknowledge with thanks permission granted by Mouton de Gruyter and Pergamon Press to reprint portions of my articles

ACKNOWLEDGEMENTS

'Aspect, foregrounding and point of view' (*Text* 7–4, 1987) and 'Cohesive devices and discourse competence' (*World Englishes* 7–2, 1988). Extracts from *Mrs Dalloway* and *To the Lighthouse* are reproduced by kind permission of the Executors of the Virginia Woolf Estate, the Hogarth Press, and Harcourt Brace Jovanovich Inc.

Finally, I thank Peter Avery, who made me feel that I wasn't working in a vacuum, and Bernie Frohmann, for his intellectual clarity and his never-failing encouragement during the various stages of preparation of this work.

Susan Ehrlich
Toronto, Canada

ABBREVIATIONS

ET = event time
NP = noun phrase
RST = represented speech and thought
RT = reference time
SCP = sentence containing parenthetical
ST = speech time
VP = verb phrase

So much depends then, thought Lily Briscoe, looking at the sea which had scarcely a stain on it, which was so soft that the sails and the clouds seemed set in its blue, so much depends, she thought, upon distance; whether people are near us or far from us; for her feeling for Mr Ramsay changed as he sailed across the bay.

(Virginia Woolf, *To the Lighthouse*)

INTRODUCTION

Of increasing interest in text linguistics and discourse analysis is the identification of linguistic properties of narrative texts responsible for their temporal organization. Labov (1972) defines a minimal narrative text as one containing at least two temporally ordered clauses (what he terms 'narrative clauses') in which the events are presented in an order that matches their occurrence in the depicted world. In addition, these temporally ordered clauses must have the effect of moving time forward in the depicted world in order to meet Labov's condition on narrativity. Labov and others have investigated the particular linguistic features that serve to signal narrative clauses or (what has also been called) the 'foreground' of a narrative. Most investigations of foreground have involved the analysis of relatively simple texts, usually short oral narratives representing events from a single viewpoint. This study departs from such studies in analysing literary narratives conveyed from a multiplicity of perspectives.

Modern literary narratives, like modern paintings, are often represented from different viewing positions. In the case of a painting, the differing viewpoints will vary in terms of spatial position; in the case of a narrative, the differing viewpoints may vary both spatially and temporally. The texts investigated in this study are narratives characterized by frequent shifts in the spatial and temporal positions from which events and descriptions are related. The examples that constitute the data-base of this book come from two novels by Virginia Woolf, *To the Lighthouse* and *Mrs Dalloway*. Auerbach (1968) makes the following comments regarding the multiplicity of perspectives, emblematic of Woolf's style:

POINT OF VIEW

The essential characteristic of the technique represented by Virginia Woolf is that we are given not merely one person whose consciousness (that is, the impressions it receives) is rendered, but many persons, with frequent shifts from one to another. . . . The design of a close approach to objective reality by means of numerous subjective impressions received by various individuals (and at various times) is important in the modern technique which we are examining. It basically differentiates it from the unipersonal subjectivism which allows only a single and generally a very unusual person to make himself heard and admits only that one person's way of looking at reality.

(Auerbach 1968: 536)

As a discourse analysis of two literary texts, this book is necessarily interdisciplinary. Its purpose is twofold. From the perspective of linguistics, it seeks to analyse the discourse structure of texts with a complex temporal organization. From the perspective of literary studies, it seeks to explain certain non-linguistic aspects of the texts, i.e. point of view, in terms of linguistic form. This book, then, extends the domain of discourse analysis to include the language of complex literary texts and, at the same time, offers a descriptively adequate account of the relationship between linguistic form and point of view. Inasmuch as the central aim of this study is to make explicit the linguistic clues that readers use in identifying point of view, my goal is *not* to provide new 'readings' of the texts under investigation. Because point of view interpretations do not differ radically from reader to reader, the analysis of point of view in literary narratives constitutes a natural intersection for the disciplines of linguistics and literary studies. By focusing on the formal linguistic properties of literary texts, I do not offer new interpretations of these texts but rather attempt to *explain* readers' interpretations of certain aspects of the texts (i.e. point of view).

The book is organized as follows. Chapter 1 demonstrates the limitations of previous linguistic accounts of point of view, arguing that reference to discourse properties of texts is essential to a more satisfactory account. Chapter 2 describes my linguistic framework for cohesion and coherence. Chapters 3 and 4 show that the interpretation of point of view is related to three discourse conditions of cohesion: referential linking, semantic connector linking, and temporal linking. In Chapter 5, I demonstrate the relationship

INTRODUCTION

between aspectual distinctions and coherence, on the one hand, and the interpretation of point of view, on the other. Chapter 6 summarizes the major points made in previous chapters by analysing several extended pieces of text, and then considers the literary function of linguistic correlates of point of view above the level of the sentence. In Chapter 7, I discuss the implications of my analysis for linguistic studies of foreground and background.

Within the framework developed in this book, sentences that are locally cohesive and/or coherent with previous discourse are shown to be interpreted in a similar fashion in terms of point of view. Conversely, sentences that lack local cohesion and/or coherence with previous discourse are shown to be interpreted differently in terms of point of view. The analysis has implications for recent work in discourse analysis concerned with the temporal organization of narrative texts. Such investigations have attempted to isolate the linguistic features of texts that correlate with foreground and background material (i.e. linguistic material that serves to move a narrative through time as opposed to linguistic material that serves to elaborate upon and embellish the main story line of a narrative). This book demonstrates that the simple binary distinction between foreground and background is not completely adequate for describing texts conveyed from multiple points of view. Texts such as these must be viewed as containing foreground and background material represented from various viewpoints. In addition, it is demonstrated that 'traditional' correlates of foreground and background, such as the perfective/imperfective aspectual alternation, cannot be explained exclusively in terms of these discourse functions.

Throughout the book, references to primary novels are cited by title and page: for example, *To the Lighthouse*, 86–9, and *Mrs Dalloway*, 202. The editions are those of the Hogarth Press reprinted by Penguin books. Occasionally, cited texts and variants of texts are accompanied by marks indicating either grammaticality or pragmatic judgements. The symbol '*' in a single-sentence example indicates ungrammaticality and within a context indicates pragmatic inappropriateness. The symbol '#' indicates semantic deviance. Italicized phrases and clauses in the cited texts are my own, unless otherwise indicated.

1

SENTENCE-BASED APPROACHES TO POINT OF VIEW

1.0 INTRODUCTION

The question of whose point of view a speaker/writer adopts in describing events within a narrative has been the subject of much study in the field of literary criticism.[1] In recent years, it has received attention from linguists who have argued that linguistic form contributes to the apprehension of point of view. That is, a reader/listener will interpret an utterance or discourse as reflecting a particular point of view, in part, because of the linguistic form of that utterance or discourse. Kuno and Kaburaki (1975), for example, show how certain formal properties of a sentence can affect its interpretation in terms of point of view. Sentences with the same propositional content, like those in (1) below, differ with respect to what Kuno and Kaburaki call 'camera angles'.

(1)   a. John hit Mary.
      b. John hit his wife.
      c. Mary's husband hit her.

In (1a), the event in question is presented objectively by the speaker; the camera can be said to be placed at some point equi-distant from both John and Mary. In (1b), the speaker describes the event from John's point of view, and in (1c) from Mary's point of view. In (1b), Kuno and Kaburaki claim that the camera is placed closer to John in viewing the event and in (1c) that the camera is placed closer to Mary. What is crucial to notice is that the linguistic form of these sentences determines these differing interpretations.

Building on the work of Kuno and Kaburaki, Kuno (1987) substitutes the term 'empathy' for the notion of 'camera angle', defining empathy as 'the speaker's identification, which may vary in degree, with a person/thing that participates in the event or state that he describes in a sentence' (Kuno 1987: 206). For Kuno, syntactic constructions differ to the extent that they convey a speaker's empathy. A passive sentence like *Bill was hit by his brother*, for example, is said to convey a speaker's closer identification with *Bill* than with John (the referent of *his brother*). On the other hand, the active sentence *John hit his brother* is said to convey the opposite empathy perspective. (These interpretations are also a result of the possessive NPs, which indicate that the speaker is closer to the referent of the possessor than to that of the entire NP.)

While Kuno distinguishes between the linguistic correlates of partial and total identification of the speaker with a person or character being described, he points out that the latter perspective seldom occurs in conversation but readily occurs in narratives. Kuroda (1973), for example, identifies a narrative style in Japanese (what he calls a non-reportive style) where, in Kuno's terms, the narrator (speaker) totally identifies with the characters involved in the described events. Of linguistic interest within this style is the co-occurrence of sensation adjectives, normally predicated of first-person subjects, with third-person subjects. Because the sensation adjectives in question can represent only a speaker's *experiencing* of sensations or emotions, their occurrence with third-person subjects serves to invoke the third person's point of view. Thus, in Kuno's terms, the narrator (speaker) totally identifies with the third person.

Kuroda's non-reportive style has an English counterpart in what has been termed free, indirect style.[2] Like the non-reportive style of Japanese, free, indirect style often exhibits the narrator's (speaker's) total identification with characters. That is, the subjective points of view of third-person subjects often emerge within texts characterized by free, indirect style. Several linguistic treatments (Banfield 1973, 1978, 1981, 1982; Fillmore 1981; Dry 1975, 1977) of this style have attempted to describe the causal relationship that exists between certain linguistic phenomena and the interpretation of point of view. While these studies have gone a long way in establishing the linguistic correlates of point of view, it is my contention that they have not been completely adequate in accounting for point of view in free, indirect style because they are sentence-based analyses. In this chapter, I point out some of the limitations of a strictly syntactic account of point of view and suggest that an analysis that goes beyond the level of the sentence is a more descriptively adequate one. In the sections that follow, I present a general description of free, indirect style (exemplified by passages from Woolf), a discussion of the limitations of previous linguistic treatments, and a discussion of the style in relation to the discourse notions of foreground and background.

1.1 GENERAL DESCRIPTION

Following Banfield, I will refer to the literary style under discussion as represented speech and thought (hereafter RST). The formal distinctiveness of this style lies in its blurring of the distinction between direct and indirect discourse. While displaying many of the features of direct discourse, the sentences of RST maintain the pronominal reference and the sequence of tense that characterizes indirect discourse.

Traditionally such texts have been classified as 'third-person narratives' because the narrator or formal speaker of the discourse never speaks of himself/herself but rather of characters designated by third-person pronouns. In such texts, then, there is an absence of first-person pronouns which designate the formal speaker of the discourse. 'Third-person narratives' have traditionally been distinguished from 'first-person narratives' in that the latter do contain 'first-person pronouns which refer to the narrator/formal speaker of the discourse. In fact, the terms 'third-person narrative' and 'first-person narrative' are misnomers, as they imply the complete absence of first-person pronouns within 'third-person narratives'. It is possible for texts traditionally labelled as 'third-person narratives' to contain first-person pronouns in direct discourse where the first-person pronoun refers to a character in the text. Tamir (1976) suggests replacing the inadequate terminology 'first and third-person narration' by personal and impersonal discourse, respectively. If the narrator/formal speaker of a text refers to himself/herself (i.e. if the narrator is a participant in the events he/she is narrating), then the text is considered to be personal discourse, according to Tamir. If, on the other hand, the narrator/formal speaker does not refer to himself/herself in the discourse, then the text is considered to be impersonal discourse.

In RST, the narrator/formal speaker does not speak of himself/ herself but rather reports on the activities, thoughts, and speech of characters in the fictional world. What distinguishes RST from other styles of impersonal discourse is the fact that many direct discourse constructions appear in the reporting (i.e. indirect discourse) of characters' thoughts and speech. In other words, rather than reporting the thoughts and/or speech of characters from an objective perspective, the narrator reports them almost as they are spoken or thought by the characters themselves. In Kuno's terms, the narrator totally identifies with a character in viewing the events of the narrative.

The effect of the mixture of direct and indirect discourse in texts characterized by RST is the emergence of points of view that do not always correspond to the point of view of the narrator of the discourse (i.e. a point of view where the speaker is equi-distant from all characters). This is impersonal discourse, then, because the narrator never speaks of himself/herself; however, this is impersonal discourse in which the personal perspectives of characters can be discerned. Auerbach (1968) has called RST and Woolf's prose, in particular, 'a multi-personal representation of consciousness' because the events of the narrative are conveyed from the perspective of many different characters within the fictional world as well as of the narrator.

Consider the RST passage below from *To the Lighthouse* which illustrates the mixture of direct and indirect discourse. Notice, especially, that two formal properties of indirect discourse – concordance of grammatical person and concordance of tense – are evident. The sentences are indexed [a], [b], etc. for ease of reference.

(2)   [a] Wasn't it late? she asked. [b] They hadn't come home yet. [c] He flicked his watch carelessly open. [d] But it was only just past seven. [e] He held his watch open for a moment, deciding that he would tell her what he had felt on the terrace. [f] To begin with, it was not reasonable to be so nervous. [g] Andrew could look after himself. [h] Then, he wanted to tell her that when he was walking on the terrace just now – here he became uncomfortable, as if he were breaking into that solitude, that aloofness, that remoteness of hers. . . . [i] But she pressed him. [j] What had he wanted to tell her, she asked, thinking it was about going to the Lighthouse; and that he was sorry he had said 'Damn you'. [k] But no. [l] He did not like to see her look so sad, he said. [m] Only wool gathering, she protested, flushing a little.

(*To the Lighthouse*, 78–9)

Concordance of grammatical person is exemplified in sentence [l] where the referent, Mr Ramsay, is designated by a third-person pronoun in both the main and embedded clauses: *He did not like to see her look so sad, he said*. Direct discourse requires no such concordance of grammatical person as it reports actual speech events. For example, the direct discourse counterpart of [l] might be: 'I don't like to see you look so sad,' he said. Thus, in direct discourse co-referential NPs are always designated by different person pronouns ('I' and 'he', in this example) in the main and embedded clauses.

Concordance of tense is exemplified in sentence [j]: *What had he wanted to tell her, she asked.* The verb of the embedded clause (past perfect) differs in tense from the verb of the speech event (simple past). In the direct discourse counterpart of [j], 'What did you want to tell me,' she asked, both verbs are in the simple past. In sentence [j], the verb of the embedded clause has been back-shifted to past perfect in order to agree with the past tense of the narrative time-line.

While this passage displays these two formal markers of indirect discourse, it also contains formal features of direct discourse. Sentence [j] contains an inverted question, a syntactic structure ordinarily restricted to direct discourse as indicated by the ungrammaticality of (3):

(3)   *She asked what had he wanted to tell her.[3]

Inverted questions are, of course, permissible in direct discourse as direct discourse reports the actual words a speaker utters. Sentence [m] exemplifies another construction normally restricted to direct discourse, an incomplete sentence (*Only wool gathering, she protested*). The indirect discourse counterpart would be the ungrammatical sentence:

(4)   *She protested (that) only wool gathering.

Other syntactic structures of direct discourse can be found in the passages below. (Notice that both of these passages show concordance of grammatical person and tense.)

(5)   He was really, Lily Briscoe thought, in spite of his eyes, but then look at his nose, look at his hands, the most uncharming human being she had ever met.
      (*To the Lighthouse*, 99)

(6)   What he would have liked, she supposed, would have been to say how he had been to Ibsen with the Ramsays. He was an awful prig – oh yes, an insufferable bore. For, though they had reached the town now and were in the

main street, with carts grinding past on the cobbles, still he went on talking, about settlements, and teaching, and working men, and helping our own class, and lectures till she gathered that he had got back entire self-confidence, had recovered from the circus. . . .

(*To the Lighthouse*, 15–16)

In (5), the exclamatory sentence, *but then look at his nose, look at his hands*, occurs in the reporting of Lily's thought. This type of expression is normally excluded from indirect discourse, as exemplified by (7):

(7) *Lily Briscoe thought (that) but then look at his nose, look at his hands.

Passage (8) contains another exclamation, *oh yes, an insufferable bore*, which can only be attributed to Mrs Ramsay's consciousness even though it is not directly embedded under a higher verb of speech or thought. Again, notice that such exclamations are ordinarily excluded from indirect discourse.

(8) *She thought (that) he was an awful prig – oh yes, an insufferable bore.

In attempting to characterize the effect of interspersing direct discourse constructions within the broader context of indirect discourse, it may be useful to invoke Genette's distinction between 'who sees' and 'who speaks' within a narrative (Genette 1980). The 'speaker' in the examples above is not necessarily the same person who orients the narrative perspective in terms of point of view. For example, the person whose perspective is evident in a sentence like, *He was an awful prig – oh yes, an insufferable bore*, is not the narrator of the text but one of the characters, Mrs Ramsay. Her point of view orients the above sentence, yet she is not the formal speaker of this sentence, as indicated by the back-shifted tense (*was*) and the surrounding sentences in which she is designated by third-person pronouns rather than first-person pronouns.

Passages of RST often include sentences in which the person 'who speaks' and the person 'who sees' are different. On the one hand, features of indirect discourse create a formal 'speaker' who is distinct from any of the characters within the text. On the other hand, features of direct discourse create a point of view that can only be attributed to one of the characters. Several literary critics have described the function of this style as one in which a character's speech and thoughts are not just reported, but rather rendered almost verbatim (Dillon and Kirchhoff 1976; Leech and Short 1981). The narrator in these texts, implied by means of the presence of formal properties of indirect discourse, is always an intermediary between the reader and the characters' speech and thought; thus, critics perceive the style as almost rendering verbatim the speech and thoughts of characters. Rimmon-Kenan (1983) emphasizes the 'double-edged' effect of the style. While the presence of a 'speaker' distinct from the characters 'may create an ironic distancing', the direct discourse characteristics of the style 'may promote an empathetic identification on the part of the reader' (Rimmon-Kenan 1983: 114).

It should be noted at this point that while I adopt Banfield's term, represented speech and thought (RST), to describe the portions of text where the subjective impressions of characters emerge, I take a different approach from Banfield concerning the question of narrator in these texts. One of the major points of Banfield's (1973, 1978, 1981, 1982) work involves the appropriateness of the communication model as a theory of narrative. Following Hamburger (1973) and Kuroda (1973), Banfield argues that 'a text without the first-person pronoun (outside direct speech) or without any linguistic signs of the speaker ... has no narrator' (Banfield 1973:34–5). More specifically, the sentences of RST are said to be 'speakerless' because they exhibit no overt evidence of the speech event. That is, the formal speaker or narrator of such sentences never refers to himself/herself as *I*, and the addressee of the speech event, *you*, is never mentioned. Following Tamir (1976), my own approach to this question is functional rather than ontological. The texts under investigation here are impersonal in Tamir's sense because there is no evidence of the speech event. I take this to mean, however, not that the narrator does not 'exist' but rather that there is a 'speaking voice,' distinct from any characters, whose role is minimal or 'negligible' (Genette 1980) in the narration.[4] In contrast to this kind of impersonal discourse is personal discourse (Tamir 1976), where the narrator or 'speaking voice' plays an active role in the narrative events, either by pronouncing explicit judgements upon them or by entering into them. My approach to this issue is consistent with Kuno's approach to point of view or empathy whereby a *speaker* identifies to a greater or lesser degree with the characters of the narrated events.[5]

SENTENCE-BASED APPROACHES TO POINT OF VIEW

1.1.1 Sentences containing parentheticals

Some sentences of RST contain parentheticals indicating explicitly the source of the represented speech and thought, while other sentences of RST do not. In this section, I discuss the former type of sentence and in the following section (1.1.2) I discuss the latter.

Examples of sentences containing parentheticals (hereafter SCPs) that occur in texts characterized by RST are provided below:

(9)   a. Her shoes were excellent, he observed.
(To the Lighthouse, 22)

b. All these young men parodied her husband, she reflected; . . .
(To the Lighthouse, 19)

c. Something was up, she knew.
(Mrs Dalloway, 31)

d. No crime; love; he repeated, fumbling for his card and pencil. . . .
(Mrs Dalloway, 76)

e. Had he blown his brains out, they asked. . . .
(To the Lighthouse, 34)

The parentheticals do not always occur after the RST as in the examples above. They also occur interpolated within the RST, as exemplified in (10):

(10)   a. She could see the horns, Cam said, all over the room.
(To the Lighthouse, 131)

b. It was nailed fast, Mildred said, and Cam couldn't go to sleep with it in the room, and James screamed if she touched it.
(To the Lighthouse, 131)

c. Human relations were all like that, she thought, and the worst (if it had not been for Mr Bankes) were between men and women.
(To the Lighthouse, 107)

According to Reinhart (1983), SCPs are of two types. She distinguishes between SCPs that are speaker-oriented and SCPs that are parenthetical-subject-oriented. The two kinds differ with respect to whose point of view is represented and display different formal properties. Consider sentences (11) and (12) below (from Reinhart 1983:175):

(11)　He$_i$ would be late, John$_i$ said.
(12)　John$_i$ will be late, he$_i$ said.

In uttering (11), it is necessary that John said something very similar to 'I will be late' or the sentence is false. With (12), however, the speaker is asserting that John will be late without necessarily entailing that John uttered 'I will be late'. The speaker could have inferred this assertion from anything John said. Reinhart (1983:175) claims that, in its force, a sentence like (12) does not differ significantly from (13):

(13)　John will be late, I think.

Sentence (11), then, is an SCP representing parenthetical-subject point of view while sentence (12) is an SCP representing speaker point of view (speaker of the utterance). The truth conditions for the two types of SCPs are different. In order that a parenthetical-subject-oriented SCP be true, it is necessary that the parenthetical-subject said or believed something very similar to the main clause. In order that a speaker-oriented SCP be true, it is only necessary that the speaker have a certain belief about the content of the main clause; it is not necessary that the parenthetical-subject said or believed the content of the main clause.

While SCPs can be speaker-oriented or parenthetical-subject-oriented, only one of these possibilities is possible in a given SCP. By contrast, sentences with embedded-*that* clauses may have two possible readings, one in which the speaker's point of view is represented and one in which the parenthetical-subject's point of view is represented. Consider this sentence from Reinhart (1983:170):

(14)　Ralph believes that Ortcutt is a spy.

In one possible reading, the speaker of the utterance (or narrator) is using Ortcutt to refer to the man in question and Ralph is unaware of his name (speaker's point of view); in the other, Ralph has referred to this person as Ortcutt (Ralph's point of view). Sentence (15), also a sentence with an embedded-*that* clause, has only one plausible reading.

(15)　Oedipus believed that his mother wasn't his mother.

The reading representing Oedipus' point of view (parenthetical-subject point of view) is contradictory as it requires claiming that Oedipus believes something like 'my mother is not my mother'. The other reading, in which the speaker uses one of the occurrences of 'his mother' to refer to Jocasta, is non-contradictory (speaker point of view).

As evidence that SCPs allow only one reading, consider (16) below. It is semantically deviant because it requires saying that Oedipus believes a contradiction; i.e. that his mother is not his mother.

(16) #His mother was not his mother, Oedipus believed.

This semantic deviance indicates, first of all, that the SCP allows only one point of view (the non-contradictory reading is not possible) and, secondly, that the point of view represented is that of the parenthetical subject, Oedipus.

The unambiguous interpretations that SCPs allow, with respect to point of view, are of two kinds: parenthetical-subject-oriented and speaker-oriented. Corresponding to the differences in point of view displayed by the two types of SCPs (as in (11) and (12) above) are differences in the formal characteristics of the sentences. In parenthetical-subject-oriented SCPs, as in (11) above, Reinhart argues that backward pronominalization and tense agreement are obligatory. In speaker-oriented SCPs, as in (12) above, forward pronominalization is obligatory and the tense of the main clause is determined in relation to real time. Reinhart provides the following sentences to exemplify the differences between the two types of SCPs with respect to tense and anaphora:

(17) a. He_i would be late for her_j party, $John_i$ told $Mary_j$.
      b. *$John_i$ would be late for $Mary's_j$ party, he_i told her_j.
      c. $John_i$ will be late for $Mary's_j$ party, he_i told her_j.

Sentence (17a) displays backward pronominalization and concordance of tense between the main clause and the parenthetical clause. According to Reinhart, (17a) reports some actual speech event in which John addressed Mary and, consequently, is a parentheticalsubject-oriented SCP. Sentence (17c), on the other hand, displays forward pronominalization and does not show concordance of tense. It represents an assertion of the speaker which does not necessarily correspond to some speech event in which John addressed Mary. It is a speaker-oriented SCP.

The sentences containing parentheticals that occur in RST are parenthetical-subject-oriented SCPs. As has been shown above, the SCPs within RST show concordance of tense, just as main and subordinate clauses do in indirect discourse. The following sentences provide further examples of this agreement of tense in SCPs within RST:

(18) a. He had spent his honeymoon on the banks of the Kennet, he said.
(To the Lighthouse, 62)

b. She had been reading fairy tales to James, she said.
(To the Lighthouse, 79)

c. She had had to buy the roses, Rezia said, from a poor man in the street.
(Mrs Dalloway, 103)

d. He had four little children and he had asked her to tea, she told Septimus.
(Mrs Dalloway, 102)

The SCPs in RST also display backward pronominalization:

(19) a. She$_i$ knew all about *that*, said Mrs Ramsay$_i$.
(To the Lighthouse, 77)

b. He$_i$'d disinherit her if she married him, said Mr Ramsay$_i$.
(To the Lighthouse, 77)

c. Her$_i$ Aunt Camilla was far worse than she was, Mrs Ramsay$_i$ remarked.
(To the Lighthouse, 78)

d. When he$_i$ felt like that he went to the Music Hall, said Dr Holmes$_i$.
(Mrs Dalloway, 100–1)

The formal properties of SCPs within RST, then, correspond to the formal properties of parenthetical-subject-oriented SCPs. It is not surprising that the SCPs within RST are SCPs of this type, given the formal and functional characteristics of RST already discussed. We have seen that RST displays many of the syntactic constructions of direct speech: inverted questions, incomplete sentences, and exclamatory sentences. These direct discourse constructions are appropriate in parenthetical-subject-oriented SCPs precisely because these SCPs represent the content of characters' speech or thought from the parenthetical-subject's point of view (i.e. the character's point of view).

SENTENCE-BASED APPROACHES TO POINT OF VIEW

1.1.2 Sentences not containing parentheticals

Not all sentences of RST contain parentheticals indicating explicitly the source of the speech or thought. In passage (6), for example, the sentence, *He was an awful prig – oh yes, an insufferable bore*, does not contain a parenthetical. Yet it seems clear that this sentence is a representation of a thought of Mrs Ramsay's owing to the presence of the exclamation *oh yes* and the lexical items *awful prig*, locutions that the reader recognizes as characteristic of Mrs Ramsay. More significantly, the preceding sentence in the passage is an SCP, attributing the source of the thought to Mrs Ramsay. Further examples of RST sentences without parentheticals can be seen in the following passage:

(20) He was not going to be condescended to by these silly women. He had been reading in his room, and now he came down and it all seemed to him silly, superficial, flimsy. Why did they dress? He had come down in his ordinary clothes. He had not got any dress clothes. 'One never gets anything worth having by post' – that was the sort of thing they were always saying. They made men say that sort of thing. Yes, it was pretty well true, he thought. They never got anything worth having from one year's end to another. They did nothing but talk, talk, talk, eat, eat, eat. It was the women's fault. Women made civilization impossible with all their 'charm', all their silliness.

(*To the Lighthouse*, 98–9)

There is only one sentence in this passage that contains a parenthetical: *Yes, it was pretty well true, he thought*. One other sentence in the passage specifies the source of the content of the passage (*it all seemed to him*). Other than these two sentences, however, there are no sentences in this passage that are specified as being thoughts of the character, Mr Tansley. Yet the sentences are interpreted as representations of the thoughts of this character, despite the absence of parentheticals indicating the source consciousness explicitly. In addition to parentheticals, then, direct discourse constructions such as *Why did they dress?*, lexical items such as *silly* and the repetition of lexical items in *They did nothing but talk, talk, talk, eat, eat, eat* all contribute to the interpretation of these sentences as the RST of Mr Tansley.

Further examples of parenthetical-less sentences interpreted as RST are presented below:

(21) 'Yes. She says they're building a new billiard room,' he said. *No! No! That was out of the question! Building a billiard room!* It seemed to her impossible.

(*To the Lighthouse*, 101)

(22) He said they had built a billiard room – *was it possible? Would William go on talking about the Mannings?* She wanted him to. *But no* – for some reason he was no longer in the mood.

(*To the Lighthouse*, 107)

(23) ... – one feels in the midst of the traffic, or waking at night, Clarissa was positive, a particular hush ... before Big Ben strikes. *There! Out it boomed.*

(*Mrs Dalloway*, 6)

In (21), the italicized sentences do not contain parentheticals indicating that the sentences represent the thought of the referent of *her*, but the italicized expressive elements (i.e. *No! No! That was out of the question! Building a billiard room!*) cause them to be interpreted as RST. Similarly, in (22), the combination of the expressive element *But no* and the sentences that have undergone subject–auxiliary inversion (a root transformation not normally occurring in indirect discourse) invoke the subjective viewpoint of the referent of *she*, Mrs Ramsay. Example (23) contains further examples of expressive elements that contribute to their sentences' interpretation as RST.

Sentences representing the speech and thought of characters, then, do not necessarily contain parentheticals indicating explicitly that they represent the consciousness of a character. Other formal features of these sentences (e.g. direct discourse constructions, exclamatory expressions, and root transformations) contribute to their being interpreted as sentences of RST rather than sentences expressing the point of view of the narrator (i.e. where the narrator assumes a position equi-distant from all characters).

1.2 LIMITATIONS OF SENTENCE-BASED APPROACHES TO RST

A limitation of previous linguistic treatments of RST is their concern with syntactic features only. While the sentences of RST discussed in the previous sections pose no problems for these analyses in accounting for their point of view interpretations, sentences without any of these explicit syntactic features of RST do. For example, a sentence such as *They never got anything worth having from one year's end to another* of (20) above displays no syntactic characteristics of RST, yet is clearly interpreted as an impression of Mr Tansley's. Because discourse context is relevant to the interpretation of point of view, previous accounts of RST have been descriptively inadequate owing to their exclusive consideration of sentence-internal linguistic features. In the following sections, I review previous treatments of RST, demonstrating their specific limitations.

1.2.1 Dry (1975, 1977)

Dry's analysis of RST attempts to identify syntactic features in Jane Austen's *Emma* that are responsible for the emergence of points of view that are not the narrator's. She distinguishes between two kinds of linguistic material within *Emma*, 'thought representation' and 'exposition.' Thought representation refers to material that is attributed to a 'source consciousness' that is not that of the narrator but that of a character designated by third-person NPs (what we have been calling RST). According to Dry, three types of syntactic constructions within *Emma* contribute to the impression that certain linguistic material reflects a source consciousness different from the formal speaker. These constructions include (1) third-person reflexive pronouns without overt antecedents within the same clause, (2) understood datives with specific referents, and (3) emotive constructions called 'expressives'.

Ordinarily, a reflexive occurring without an overt antecedent in the same clause is ungrammatical unless the reflexive is first or second person. In these cases, the 'antecedent' for these reflexives exists in the speaker or the addressee of the speech event. In *Emma*, and in RST in general, third-person reflexives occur without overt antecedents. The following example comes from Woolf:

(24) *That was one of the bonds between Sally and himself.*
There was a garden where they used to walk, a walled-in place, with rose-bushes and giant cauliflowers – he could

remember Sally tearing off a rose, stopping to exclaim at the beauty of the cabbage leaves in the moonlight (it was extraordinary how vividly it all came back to him, things he hadn't thought of for years). . . .

(*Mrs Dalloway*, 84)

Dry claims, and I think correctly, that the third-person reflexives without antecedents imply that the third person referent is the 'source consciousness' of the passage and, in this way, the italicized sentence above is understood as reflecting the point of view of the referent of *himself*.

Dry's analysis of understood datives is similar. She points out that certain VPs like *be difficult, be easy, be necessary*, etc. take a dative phrase indicating to whom or for whom the state is predicated. This dative phrase may be deleted under certain conditions in ordinary conversation, one of which exists when the dative NP is coreferential with the speaker or addressee of the speech event. Again, in *Emma* and in RST in general, these datives will be deleted when the NP designates neither the speaker nor the addressee, but a third person. The following example also comes from Woolf:

(25) If only she could put them together, she felt, write them out in some sentence, then she would have got at the truth of things. . . . *The extraordinary unreality was frightening; but it was also exciting.*

(*To the Lighthouse*, 167)

This has the same effect as the third-person reflexive without an overt antecedent in that the referent of a third-person pronoun is implied to be the source consciousness (triggering the deletion of the dative NP) and, consequently, the last sentence of this passage is perceived as representing Lily Briscoe's (the referent of *she*) point of view.

Dry's third syntactic characteristic contributing to the emergence of Emma's point of view is one that has been discussed in a previous section, expressive elements. These are constructions that are colloquial and perceived as belonging to thought or speech even in a context where thought or speech is not directly represented.

(26) She would take her silks, her scissors, her – *what was it?* – thimble, *of course*, down into the drawing-room, for she must also write, and see that things generally were more or less in order.

(*Mrs Dalloway*, 43)

The occurrence of expressive elements like *what was it?* and *of course* contribute to the emergence of a character's viewpoint as a character's words or thoughts occur in the context of indirect discourse.

Dry's other category of linguistic material, exposition, seems to include all the text that cannot be regarded as reflecting a character's perspective. It is 'everything that could not be transposed into first person and appropriately regarded as part of a character's internal sentences' (1977: 89). While it is clear that Dry is concerned with establishing the syntactic correlates of RST, her comment suggests that she believes there to be more than just syntax involved in the interpretation of sentences as RST. In other words, she does not differentiate between thought representation and exposition on the basis of syntactic characteristics alone but appeals to the 'appropriateness' of sentences as part of a character's internal thought as a way of distinguishing between the two. I agree with Dry's implication that syntactic characteristics alone cannot explain the interpretation of all sentences of RST. And, like Dry, I see the semantic content of particular sentences as a determining factor in explaining their interpretation as RST. However, I believe that there is a large set of sentences in texts characterized by RST whose interpretation as RST cannot be explained simply by semantic content and/or syntactic factors. These are sentences whose semantic content can be attributed equally as easily to a character as to the narrator and that contain none of the syntactic properties of RST discussed above.

The following examples from Woolf's texts illustrate this point. The passages contain sentences that are explicitly identified as RST by the presence of a parenthetical. These SCPs are followed by sentences that contain none of the syntactic characteristics discussed above. That is, they contain no expressive elements, no reflexives without overt antecedents, no root transformations, and no understood datives.

(27) [a] He [Mr Ramsay] would be impatient in a moment, James thought, and Cam thought, looking at their father, who sat in the middle of the boat between them (James steered; Cam sat alone in the bow) with his legs tightly curled. [b] He hated hanging about.

(*To the Lighthouse*, 184)

(28) [a] When he felt like that he went to the Music Hall, said Dr Holmes. [b] He took a day off with his wife and played golf.

(*Mrs Dalloway*, 100–1)

The [b] sentences in (27) and (28), despite the absence of any syntactic characteristics of RST, are not interpreted as exposition, as reflecting the narrator's viewpoint. Notice also that, based on their semantic content, both of the [b] sentences could plausibly be interpreted as conveying the narrator's viewpoint. However, in (27), it is not the objective narrator who relays the fact that Mr Ramsay hates hanging about. The [b] sentence is interpreted as reflecting the viewpoint of James and Cam of the preceding sentence. Similarly, in (28), it is not the narrator who is telling the reader about Dr Holmes' activities; rather, this must be attributed to the consciousness of the character, Dr Holmes. What these passages illustrate is that an analysis of RST solely in terms of syntactic characteristics cannot account for the interpretation of the [b] sentences above as part of RST.

1.2.2 Banfield (1973, 1978, 1981, 1982)

Banfield's treatment of RST, while being a more exhaustive syntactic analysis than Dry's, suffers from the same type of descriptive inadequacy as Dry's. Banfield, like Dry, distinguishes between two kinds of sentences in literary texts: sentences of RST and sentences of narration (which relate events from an objective perspective). In Banfield's terms, sentences of narration 'merely recount an event and do so objectively', whereas sentences of RST recount events 'as represented from within a consciousness' (Banfield 1982: 158). From these comments, we can see that Banfield's narration is roughly the same as Dry's exposition, in that the linguistic material of narration does not represent a character's perspective on events in the fictional world.[6] In Kuno's terms, narration would include sentences in which the formal speaker or narrator of the text is in a position equi-distant from all characters.

Like Dry, Banfield isolates syntactic characteristics that differentiate sentences of RST from sentences of narration. These syntactic characteristics are as follows: (1) choice of tense, (2) presence or absence of character-oriented deictics, and (3) presence or absence of expressive elements (i.e. exclamations, repetitions, direct questions, root transformations, subjective grammatical items, etc.). Sentences containing parentheticals are considered by Banfield to be sentences of RST with an explicit indication of the source consciousness whose point of view is being represented. Parenthetical-less sentences could potentially be interpreted either as RST or as narration. It is the formal features listed above that Banfield claims will distinguish a parenthetical-less sentence of RST from a sentence of narration and, therefore, will explain the differing interpretations of the two in terms of point of view. Each of these syntactic characteristics will be discussed in turn.

Choice of tense

The first syntactic characteristic discussed by Banfield relates to the choice of tense within a particular sentence. (What Banfield calls tense is more accurately referred to in the linguistics literature as aspect. I will follow this tradition and also refer to it as aspect.) Within French narrative texts, according to Banfield, there is an aspectual distinction between the aorist and the imparfait, which Banfield, citing Benveniste, states is correlated with narration and RST, respectively. That is, the aorist form of the verb is used for events that are related objectively and the imparfait form of the verb is used for events that are related from the viewpoint of a character. This distinction is analogous in certain cases, Banfield claims, to the simple past/past progressive alternation in English. She (1982: 105–6) provides the following examples:

(29) a. Emma looked out the window.
  b. A few drops of rain fell.
              were falling.

(30) a. She listened.
  b. A piano played.
              was playing.

Sentences (29a) and (30a) are sentences of narration. The status of (29b) and (30b) varies depending on whether the simple past or the past progressive is used. According to Banfield, the versions in the simple past are also sentences of narration; they recount events objectively. The versions in the past progressive are sentences of RST; they recount the events as they are perceived through the character's consciousness. That is, they are equivalent in terms of point of view to the sentences in (31) containing parentheticals:

(31) a. A few drops of rain were falling, she saw.
  b. A piano was playing, she thought.

Thus, for Banfield, there seems to be a one-to-one correspondence (in certain cases) between the simple past/past progressive alternation and narration/RST, respectively.

Deictics

The simple past/past progressive alternation in English is not realized with all verbs, as there is a class of verbs, known as statives, that do not ordinarily occur in the progressive. Such verbs would not display an alternation between the simple past/past progressive and, therefore, could not signal the distinction between RST and narration as far as this aspectual distinction is concerned. Banfield (1982: 157) claims that a sentence with such a verb in the simple past tense would be ambiguous in its interpretation between RST and narration, as in example (32a):

(32) a. She saw the moon.
 b. She saw the moon now.

Sentence (32b), on the other hand, is disambiguated by the presence of the time deictic *now* and can only be interpreted, according to Banfield, as representing the consciousness of the referent of *she*.

Examples of temporal and spatial deictic words that are assigned from the point of view of the character rather than the formal speaker are provided below:

(33) a. ... and of course he was coming to her party *tonight*, Evelyn absolutely insisted....
 (*Mrs Dalloway*, 8)

 b. For now she need not think about anybody. She could be herself, by herself. And that was what *now* she often felt the need of – to think; well not even to think.
 (*To the Lighthouse*, 72)

 c. Where was he *this morning* for instance? Some committee, she never asked what.
 (*Mrs Dalloway*, 10)

 d. But *now* just as she wished to say something, could have said something, perhaps, *here* they were – Cam and James.
 (*To the Lighthouse*, 175)

 e. She was trying to get *these* tiresome stockings finished to send to Sorley's little boy *tomorrow*, said Mrs Ramsay.
 (*To the Lighthouse*, 37)

This use of spatial and temporal deictics (character-oriented) was also noted by Dry (1977) as formally marking sentences of RST.

Expressive elements

Like Dry, Banfield also claims that expressive elements mark sentences as reflecting a character's consciousness. Representative examples of expressive elements have been presented in section 1.1.2 of this chapter.

For Dry and Banfield, then, certain syntactic features are responsible for a reader interpreting certain sentences or passages as being a representation of a character's thoughts or speech and others as being an objective rendering of a character's thoughts, speech, and activities. Banfield goes a step beyond Dry by formulating rules of interpretation by which certain sentences get attributed to a character's consciousness. First of all, Banfield introduces a node E(Expression) into the phrase-structure rules and a phrase-structure rule that expands Es as complete sentences or as incomplete sentences, exclamations, and/or expressive elements. Second, she formulates interpretive rules, one of which allows a third-person NP to be the 'subject of consciousness' responsible for a given E in the absence of a first-person pronoun. This third-person NP must be the subject of a parenthetical containing a consciousness verb, with the E representing the speech or thought of the parenthetical subject. The effect of this principle is to assign Es to the consciousness of the referents of third-person NPs in the absence of first-person pronouns.

We have seen, however, that not all sentences of RST have explicit parentheticals and, thus, subjects to which Es can be attributed. In such cases, Banfield states that Es must be attributed to 'an appropriate NP in a neighboring E and perhaps a consciousness or communication verb (or some other semantically related word to permit interpretation). But just which NPs are eligible and what constitutes a neighboring E has yet to be determined' (Banfield 1982: 102). In other words, Banfield is not clear about how a parenthetical-less sentence of RST gets interpreted as the speech or thought of a particular third-person NP. While Banfield's treatment of RST goes further than Dry's in providing a more complete account of the syntactic features contributing to the interpretation of point of view, it, too, has its limitations.

As has already been illustrated, Dry and Banfield have no way of accounting for the interpretation of sentences like (27b) and (28b) above, which are interpreted as RST but include none of the syntactictic features that they discuss. Notice that (28b) (*He took a day off with his wife and played golf*) contains the simple past tense; thus, a strict interpretation of Banfield's simple past and past progressive distinction and its significance in terms of point of view would suggest that this was a sentence of narration. In fact, these are back-shifted versions of the simple present tense and are interpreted as habitual events related by Dr Holmes. In (27b), we have an example of a stative verb in a sentence that is a description of Mr Ramsay. Within the context of the narrative, this sentence is interpreted as two characters' impressions of Mr Ramsay rather than as an objective fact about Mr Ramsay. Within Banfield's framework, however, it is difficult to account for this interpretation of the sentence, as the sentence contains no character-oriented deictic words and no expressive elements that would disambiguate it.

We can see, then, how Banfield's syntactic analysis of point of view is not completely adequate in explaining the interpretation of sentences as RST. As Banfield herself remarks: 'The process of reading a narrative text involves determining the status of each sentence – is its force objective and fiction-creating or must it be interpreted with the caution due any subjective statement?' (Banfield 1982: 262). It is my contention that an analysis of point of view that goes beyond the level of the sentence is necessary for determining how linguistic form contributes to the 'objective' as opposed to 'subjective' interpretations of sentences.

Banfield implies the necessity of considering discourse factors. In determining the status of two sentences from D.H. Lawrence's *Lady Chatterly's Lover*, she looks to the immediately preceding sentence in the text in order to establish that the two sentences reflect the opinion of Lady Chatterly and are, thus, sentences of RST. What Banfield demonstrates with this example is the relevance of context or discourse to the interpretation of sentences as RST or narration.

1.2.3 Fillmore (1981)

Fillmore (1981), like Dry and Banfield, distinguishes between two kinds of linguistic material in texts characterized by RST, which he calls 'thought-representing' portions and 'descriptive' portions. (These categories correspond to Dry's thought representation and exposition and Banfield's RST and narration, respectively.) Like them, Fillmore also attempts to account for the differences between these two kinds of linguistic material in terms of point of view by analysing linguistic properties of the representative texts, but Fillmore's treatment goes beyond the level of the sentence. For example, Fillmore points out that, often within RST, people and things that are known to the character whose consciousness is being represented are designated with pronouns, definite NPs, or personal names even though the reader may not yet have been introduced to these NPs. In other words, these NPs are treated as given information even though they are new information within the text (i.e. they have not been previously mentioned or implied). This type of definite reference has the effect of conveying the character's perception of these NPs, as it is only the character to whom these NPs are known or given information. If such NPs were introduced into these texts by the normal rules of discourse, they would initially be presented as indefinite, as they would be new from the perspective of the reader. For our purposes, what is noteworthy about Fillmore's observations is the fact that sentences containing new NPs linguistically marked as given information may not contain any of Dry or Banfield's syntactic characteristics of RST. Therefore, the suggestion of Dry and Banfield's analyses is that such sentences should not be interpreted as RST. Fillmore's work elucidates certain discourse properties of RST texts that are essential to a more empirically adequate account of this literary style. In looking beyond the sentence, Fillmore takes a position similar to the one I will develop in succeeding chapters.

1.3 RST/NARRATION AND FOREGROUND/BACKGROUND

One of the issues that arises out of a discussion of point of view in these literary texts is the relationship between RST and narration and the discourse notions of foreground and background. Banfield seems to equate narration with foreground material and RST with background material. Her definitions of narration are strongly reminiscent of definitions of foreground that appear in the discourse analysis literature (Hopper 1979; Reinhart 1984). In these studies, foreground material within a narrative text is defined as the material that serves to move a narrative through time, while background material is durative and descriptive material that serves to embellish and elaborate upon the foreground. Labov (1972) also equates foreground with narration to the extent that he refers to clauses that contain events on the main temporal axis of a narrative as 'narrative clauses'.[7] Additionally, Labov maintains that, in narrative clauses, events must be presented in an order that matches their order of occurrence in the represented world. Banfield states that sentences of narration 'hold the essence of the narrative' and 'narrate events'. 'These events are set forth chronologically, as they occurred' (Banfield 1982: 64).

Another similarity between Banfield's narration/RST and the foreground/background distinction in discourse analysis is her claim, as discussed previously, that the aorist/imparfait aspectual distinction in French and the simple past/past progressive distinction in English correspond to narration/RST, respectively. This particular aspectual distinction in English and French has been reported in the discourse analysis literature to signal the difference between foreground and background linguistic material (Hopper 1979; Dry 1981, 1983; Chvany 1984).

However, as we have seen in section 1.2.2, Banfield discusses other aspects of narration and RST that have nothing to do with narrative present and/or the movement of time in narrative texts. She defines sentences of narration as those 'which merely recount an event and do so objectively' and sentences of RST as recounting events 'as represented from within a consciousness' (Banfield 1982: 158). The emphasis here is on the objective/subjective nature of the linguistic material contained within sentences.

The question that arises is whether it is correct to equate foreground material with 'objective' material and background material with 'subjective' material in these narratives with multiple points of view. Is it the case, for example, that linguistic material relayed from a narrator's perspective will necessarily serve to move a narrative through time? And is it the case that linguistic material presented from a character's point of view will necessarily be durative, descriptive material that embellishes and elaborates upon the main story line of the narrative rather than advancing it? In the following chapters, I attempt to establish how points of view are successfully maintained beyond the scope of a single sentence. At the same time, I will be investigating the relationship between the discourse function of linguistic material in these texts (i.e. foreground vs. background) and the point of view from which the material is conveyed.

2

COHESION, COHERENCE, AND EPISODES

2.0 INTRODUCTION

The question that will be addressed in the next four chapters concerns the discourse means by which sentences, not internally marked as RST, come to be interpreted as such. In other words, how is it that a point of view other than the speaker's/narrator's emerges from sentences that contain none of the sentence-internal characteristics of RST discussed in Chapter 1? In this chapter, I set out the discourse framework within which my data will be analysed. I suggest, following van Dijk (1982) and van Dijk and Kintsch (1983), that fragments of discourse conveyed from different points of view be considered as separate discourse units or episodes.

That texts are more than just an undifferentiated sequence of sentences is a position held by many discourse analysts (Longacre 1979; Hinds 1979; van Dijk 1982; van Dijk and Kintsch 1983; Fox 1987; Tomlin 1987). Van Dijk (1982), for example, argues that between the unit of the sentence and the unit of the text or conversation exists a further unit of analysis, which he calls the episode:

> Roughly speaking, paragraphs or episodes are characterized as coherent sequences of sentences of a discourse, linguistically marked for beginning and/or end, and further defined in terms of identical participants, time, location or global event or action.
>
> (van Dijk 1982: 177)

According to van Dijk (1982) and van Dijk and Kintsch (1983), an episode has semantic unity or coherence (i.e. it is dominated by what van Dijk and Kintsch term a macroproposition) and will often be introduced in a 'semantically conspicuous way'. Included among the devices that may identify the beginning of a new episode are the following topic change markers:

1. Change of possible world: X dreamt . . .
2. Change of time or period: The next day . . .
3. Change of place
4. Introduction of new participants
5. Full noun phrase reintroduction of old participants
6. Change of perspective or point of view
7. Different predicate range (change of frame or script)
     (van Dijk and Kintsch 1983: 204)

Of interest here is the inclusion of linguistic devices (in (6) above) which serve to signal a shift in point of view. From this perspective, the sentence-internal properties of RST discussed in Chapter 1 are examples of 'change of perspective or point of view markers', with events and descriptions conveyed from different points of view belonging to different episodes. Put in van Dijk's terms, then, this book is both an investigation of the linguistic signals that serve to sustain RST units beyond the level of a single sentence and the linguistic signals that demarcate and delimit such units. By viewing the RST material of different characters as belonging to different discourse units or episodes, the following two chapters examine the extent to which grammatical markers of discourse episodes (those that serve to both sustain and delimit episodes) contribute to the interpretation of RST units and, more generally, to the interpretation of point of view.

2.1 COHERENCE

In attempting to define the concept of 'episode', a number of authors have invoked the notion of coherence. For example, in van Dijk's comments above, we notice that he characterizes an episode as a sequence of sentences exhibiting coherence. Unfortunately, the notion of coherence is almost as weakly defined as the concept of episode. Some studies of coherence view cohesion or a text's formal connectedness as a necessary (but not sufficient) condition of text well-formedness (Halliday and Hasan 1976; Gutwinski 1976; Reinhart 1980), while others (Giora 1985; Brown and Yule 1983) recognize the role of implicature (in Grice's sense, Grice 1975:28, 30) in allowing listeners and readers to impose coherence on texts that do not display explicit cohesive ties. As Brown and Yule (1983) point out, 'within chunks of language which are conventionally presented as texts, the hearer/reader will make every effort to impose a coherent interpretation, i.e. to treat the language thus presented as constituting "text"' (Brown and Yule 1983: 199). They conclude from this that it is impossible to isolate a set of formal features that will uniquely distinguish a 'text' from a randomly ordered set of sentences. In a similar approach to the study of textual coherence, Giora (1985) provides examples of text fragments that are not cohesive yet cohere. She formulates a condition for text coherence that requires that all sentences in a text fragment be related to an underlying discourse topic and, thus, she defines coherence independently of the formal properties of texts. Brown and Yule are even more extreme in their conclusion that 'texts are what hearers and readers treat as texts' (Brown and Yule 1983:199). While the evidence for excluding formal conditions of coherence is compelling (i.e. the existence of innumerable coherent texts with no explicit cohesive ties), the very absence of such formal features leaves us with extremely vague criteria for determining whether a text fragment is locally coherent and, concomitantly, whether it constitutes an episode.[1]

Given the difficulty in delineating precise criteria for textual coherence, for the purposes of my investigation I make a distinction between explicit and implicit coherence, following Reinhart (1980). For Reinhart, explicitly coherent texts are those that meet her three conditions for coherence: cohesion, consistency, and relevance. First of all, sentences within an explicitly coherent text must be formally connected or cohesive. Second, they must adhere to a semantic condition of consistency which requires that each sentence be consistent with previous sentences in the text (i.e. true in the same state of affairs). And third, sentences must be relevant to the underlying discourse theme of a text as well as to the context of the utterance. Implicitly coherent texts are those that are not well formed within her framework, i.e. do not meet these three conditions, but may be interpreted as coherent by means of certain interpretive procedures. These interpretive procedures would include, for example, interpreting some fragment of a text figuratively in order to impose coherence on the text as a whole. Reinhart argues that, by defining very narrowly the set of explicitly coherent texts in a language, one can begin to be more precise about the interpretive procedures by which readers impose coherence on texts that are not explicitly coherent.

POINT OF VIEW

In determining how the point of view of unmarked sentences of RST is identified by readers, I have suggested that inter-sentential linguistic features must be considered. In the remainder of this chapter, I examine the formal properties of explicitly coherent texts (i.e. cohesion) in order to establish how particular points of view can be maintained across sentence boundaries.

2.2 EXPLICIT COHERENCE: COHESION

Cohesion is defined by Reinhart (1980) as the formal connectedness of sentences within a text. As stated above, Reinhart sees cohesion as a necessary (but not sufficient) condition for a text's being globally coherent. Other conditions that Reinhart deems as necessary are consistency and relevance. In exemplifying her condition for consistency, Reinhart provides an excerpt from a schizophrenic's speech in which the speaker says that her father is dead and, in the following sentence, that he is smoking a pipe. Reinhart points out that the two utterances are formally connected in that they both contain NPs referring to the speaker's father. However, the sentences violate the condition for consistency, and therefore are not ultimately coherent, because they cannot both be true given what we know about the world. In exemplifying the condition for relevance, Reinhart provides Grice's famous example in which a professor is asked to evaluate the scholarly ability of a student. The professor responds that 'The student has clear handwriting and he has never been late to class'. This response is cohesive with previous discourse as both sentences contain NPs referring to the student in question. The response is consistent, i.e. true in the same state of affairs, as such qualities are not incompatible with either brilliant scholarship or bad scholarship. The response, however, is not relevant to the question, particularly within the context in which it is asked. Therefore, special interpretive procedures are needed in order to interpret the response as coherent with the previous discourse; thus, in Reinhart's terms, the sequence is not *explicitly* coherent.[2]

In order for sentences to be formally connected or cohesive, there are certain conditions that the relevant sentences must meet. One of the ways in which Reinhart's (1980) work on cohesion differs from Halliday and Hasan's (1976) seminal treatment of the subject is her attempt to specify the minimal conditions necessary for sentences to be considered connected. Halliday and Hasan, rather than specifying what cohesive devices are minimally necessary for a text's coherence, list the various inter-sentential devices that appear in cohesive texts. Their work thus makes no predictions about the cohesion/lack of cohesion of a given set of sentences, in the same way that a taxonomy of sentence types makes no predictions about the grammaticality/ungrammaticality of a given sentence. As Reinhart points out, it is possible for some of the cohesive devices on Halliday and Hasan's list to occur in a text without necessarily imposing cohesion on that text.[3]

Reinhart specifies the following two conditions as necessary and sufficient for connectedness between sentences:

(1) A text is connected (cohesive) iff each adjacent pair of sentences is either
 1. referentially linked   [or]
 2. linked by a semantic sentence connector.
(Reinhart 1980: 168)

It is important to take note, at this point, of some of Reinhart's assumptions regarding what sentences of a text are subject to these conditions. Although (1) above requires each adjacent pair of sentences to be subject to one of the two conditions, in actual discourse it may be possible for a given sentence to be connected to a non-adjacent preceding sentence within the same segment, where segment is taken by Reinhart to be a paragraph. Sentences introducing new segments/paragraphs are not subject to the above conditions of cohesion. They are, however, subject to the consistency and relevance conditions in order that the entire text be coherent.

Returning to the actual conditions in (1), we can see that the first of Reinhart's conditions, that of referential linking, requires adjacent (assuming the modifications mentioned above) sentences to contain NPs that designate the same referent. The second of Reinhart's conditions, that of semantic connector linking, requires that sentences be connected by some semantic marker of comparison, contrast, cause and effect, exemplification, temporal relations, etc. Notice that it is not necessary for both of these conditions to be met in order that adjacent sentences be cohesive.

2.2.1 Referential Linking

What I have said up to this point is that cohesive discourse can result from the repetition of referents within adjacent sentences. The passage below illustrates referential linking:

(2) *John Lyons* was educated at St. Bede's College, Manchester, and Cambridge, where he received his bachelor's degree in 1953. *He* served in the Royal Navy as an interpreter of Russian from 1954 to 1956, then returned to Cambridge to earn his master's and doctoral degrees and to lecture in linguistics from 1961 to 1964. *He* has taught in the United States at Indiana University, UCLA, and the University of Illinois. In addition to the present volume, *he* is the author of Structural Semantics and Introduction to Theoretical Linguistics.

(cover blurb from *Noam Chomsky* by John Lyons, 1979)

The sentences in the above text are linked by the repetition of the referent, *John Lyons*, at the beginning of each sentence. In some cases, the full NP, *John Lyons*, represents this referent and, in other cases, the pronoun *he* does. Notice that in all of these sentences *John Lyons* or *he* is the topic. That is, each sentence is about the referentially linked referent, John Lyons.

Following Kuno (1972) and Reinhart (1980, 1982), I will assume that the topic of a sentence is the element of a sentence that the sentence is about.[4] This is, of course, a rather imprecise definition of the term. The term is hard to define more precisely because the topic of a sentence is often determined by a complex combination of syntactic, semantic, and contextual factors. Topic cannot be defined on the basis of syntactic structure alone because it is possible for different NPs of the same sentence to function as topics in different contexts (Reinhart 1982). For example, *Max*, of the sentence (Reinhart 1982: 3),

(3) Max saw Rosa yesterday,

will be understood as topic, if sentence (3) is uttered as the answer to the question, *Who did Max see yesterday?* On the other hand, if sentence (3) is uttered as the answer to the question, *Did anybody see Rosa yesterday?*, *Rosa* will be understood as topic. Topic, therefore, is determined to a large extent by the context in which a sentence occurs. In (2), the topics of the sentences are identical to the subjects of the sentences and this, in fact, is a tendency in simple sentences (for topic to assume subject position). There are other syntactic structures that obligatorily mark one of the NPs in the sentence as topic, regardless of discourse context. Left dislocation is one of these structures. In sentence (4), for example, the left-dislocated NP, *Fred*, would be topic regardless of the context in which the sentence appeared.

(4) As for Fred, I don't want anything more to do with him.

Returning to passage (2), notice that the cohesion that results from the referential linking of the sentences is achieved by the retaining of the topic of the previous sentence. This, however, does not seem to be a necessary condition of referential linking producing cohesive discourse (Reinhart 1980). In (5) below, the referent, *Sir Alexander Fleming*, is repeated in the second sentence in the form of the pronoun *he*, but the NP referring to Sir Alexander Fleming is not the topic of the first sentence.

(5) The first of the antibiotics was discovered by *Sir Alexander Fleming* in 1928. *He* was busy at the time investigating a certain species of germ.

(Daneš 1974: 118)

Thus, the second sentence takes as its topic a non-topic of the first sentence and cohesive discourse is the result.

The question that arises for Reinhart is whether it is any NP from S1 and any NP from S2 (assuming S1 and S2 to be adjacent sentences) that can satisfy the referential link requirement. She shows that there are restrictions on the NP of S2 and stipulates the following condition:

(6) Two sentences, S1, S2, are referentially linked if the topic or the scene-setting expression of S2 is referentially controlled by a referent mentioned in S1.[5]

(Reinhart 1980: 174)

To illustrate this condition, Reinhart provides the following type of example:

(7) a. John is well-liked. Even Rosa likes him.
b. John is well-liked. *Rosa likes even him.[6]

Notice that, in both (7a) and (7b), the same NPs are involved in the referential link; however, in (7a), *him* does not occur with *even* whereas, in (7b), *him* does occur with *even*. The semantics of a word like *even* mark the NP occurring with *even* obligatorily as a non-topic. *Even* occurs with the focused part of a sentence; that is, the part of the sentence that denotes information assumed by the speaker not to be shared by the hearer (Jackendoff 1972). Therefore, (7a) is pragmatically appropriate, i.e. cohesive, because the discourse is about John and the co-occurrence of *even* and *Rosa* is compatible with John (or *him*) being topic. In (7b), however, *even* co-occurs with *him*, marking *him* obligatorily as non-topic and *Rosa* as topic. Because the previous sentence of (7b) is about John, it is inappropriate, or incohesive, for a sentence about Rosa to follow it. In other words, the second sentence of (7b) would be more appropriate in a context where Rosa was the topic and *him* was the focus or new information. Reinhart accounts for the cohesion of (7a) and the lack of cohesion of (7b) with (6), which stipulates that the NP of S2 participating in a referential link must be topic.

Reinhart presents no restriction on the NPs of S1 that can satisfy the referential link condition. Thus, she implies that any NP of S1 can satisfy the referential link condition as long as the condition stated in (6) is met. I have argued elsewhere (Ehrlich 1988, forthcoming) that there is also a restriction on the first NP involved in the referential link. Specifically, I demonstrate that the second NP of a referential link must be coreferential with an NP of a *dominant* clause of S1 in order for cohesive discourse to result.

2.2.2 Dominance and cohesion

Following Erteschik-Shir and Lappin (1979), I assume dominance to refer to that part of a sentence to which a speaker/writer intends to direct the hearer/reader's attention. More formally, Erteschik-Shir and Lappin provide the following definition:

(8) A constituent c, of a sentence S, is dominant in S if and only if the speaker intends to direct the attention of his/her hearer(s) to the intention of c, by uttering S.

Erteschik-Shir and Lappin (1979, 1983) have developed a 'lie-test' for determining the dominance possibilities of a sentence. This test transforms a constituent into the topic of the immediately succeeding discourse and, in this way, determines the possibility of directing a hearer's attention to that constituent. Consider the following discourse, in which the hearer responds to the speaker's sentence by picking out two different constituents as topics:

(9) Speaker: John believes that Ortcutt is a spy.
Hearer: a. That's a lie, he doesn't!
b. That's a lie, he isn't!

The fact that both the matrix and embedded clauses can be denied in the example above indicates that both of these constituents can serve as the topic for future discourse. In other words, in uttering the original sentence of (9), it is possible for the hearer's attention to be directed to either the matrix or the embedded clause. Both clauses are potentially dominant in this example.

Erteschik-Shir and Lappin note that discourse context determines, to a large extent, whether a constituent is interpreted as dominant or not. Therefore, in example (9), it will be the specific discourse context that determines which of these constituents is actually realized as dominant. Consider (10) and (11) below:

(10)   a. John$_i$ believes Ortcutt is a spy.
       b. He$_i$ also believes that his own mother is a spy.

(11)   a. John believes Ortcutt$_i$ is a spy.
       b. He$_i$ was seen entering the Soviet embassy at midnight last night.

Sentences (10b) and (11b) are both pragmatically appropriate either as responses by the hearer or as addenda by the speaker. Notice that (10b) is about some part of the original sentence's matrix clause while (11b) is about some part of the original sentence's embedded clause. The discourse context of (10) causes the matrix sentence to be realized as dominant; the discourse context of (11) causes the embedded clause to be realized as dominant.

Not all clausal constituents within multi-clausal sentences are potentially dominant. That is, there are particular syntactic structures that seem to disallow dominant readings regardless of discourse context. Erteschik-Shir and Lappin claim that syntactic islands (Ross 1967) are generally not potentially dominant constituents.[7] The following example illustrates the pragmatic inappropriateness that results when the content of a relative clause (a complex NP island) becomes the topic of the immediately succeeding discourse:

(12)   Speaker: I saw the man who was reading the *Times* yesterday and invited him home for dinner.
       Hearer: *Oh, but I can't stand the *Times*. Their editorials are so conservative.

Example (12) shows that the speaker is attempting to direct his/her hearer's attention not to the fact that the man was reading the *New York Times* (the content of the relative clause) but rather to the fact that he/she saw the man and invited him home for dinner (the content of the conjoined matrix clause). A response that concerns some other constituent of the matrix clause, which is a potentially dominant constituent, is pragmatically appropriate, as illustrated in (13):

(13) Speaker: I saw the man who was reading the *Times* yesterday and invited him home for dinner.
Hearer: Oh, I can't stand that man. He's so conservative.

Other syntactic islands that seem to disallow dominant readings, regardless of discourse context, include object complements (14), subject complements (15), and conjuncts (16):

(14) Bill said: John carefully considered the possibility that Ortcutt is a spy.
 a. which is a lie, he didn't (consider it carefully).
 b. *which is a lie, he isn't (a spy).

(15) Bill said: That Peter likes ice-cream is known by everyone.
 a. which is a lie, it isn't.
 b. *which is a lie, he doesn't.

(16) Bill said: The nurse polished her trombone and the plumber computed my tax.
 Mary said: It's a lie – a. *she didn't.
 b. *he didn't.
 c. they didn't.
 d. she did, but he didn't.

In coordinate structures such as (16) above, both conjuncts are equally dominant. Thus, one conjunct cannot be made the topic of future discourse without the other.

Expressed in terms of cohesion, the inappropriate responses in examples such as (12) and (14)–(16) can be said to be incohesive with previous discourse because they take as their topic an NP contained within a non-dominant clause of the previous utterance. Examples from single-author texts illustrate the same phenomenon:

(17) The antibiotic which was discovered by Sir Alexander Fleming caused a great disturbance in the medical community. *He was busy at the time investigating a certain species of germ.

The two sentences of (17) are referentially linked in the sense that the second sentence contains a referent that is also mentioned in the first sentence. However, when contrasted with the comparable discourse of (5), (17) seems pragmatically odd, i.e. incohesive. What is similar about (5) and (17) is the fact that the NP of S2 forming the referential link with S1 is the same for both sentences, i.e. the topic of S2 *he*. Therefore, the incohesion of (17) cannot be attributed to some fact about the coreferential NP of S2 (especially since it meets the condition in (6)). Rather, the incohesion of (17) results from the referentially linked NP of S1 being contained in a non-dominant clausal constituent, a relative clause.[8] Thus, Reinhart's condition on referential linking, shown in (6) above, must be revised as follows:

(18) Two sentences, S1, S2 are referentially linked if topic or scene-setting expression of S2 is referentially controlled by a referent mentioned in S1 and the controlling referent in S1 is contained within a dominant clause.[9]

As further evidence for this restriction on the NP of S1 participating in a referential link, I examine other syntactic structures that have been shown to be non-dominant. The test I use to establish referential linking involves an NP in S2 that has the grammatical potential of referring to either an NP in the dominant clause of S1 or an NP in the non-dominant clause of S1. Because the potentially ambiguous NP of S2 is more naturally interpreted as referring to, or forming a referential link with, the NP of the dominant clause of S1, I argue that this is further evidence for the condition stated in (18).

(19) *Complex NPs*
    a. Speaker: A man who lives with another man is running for office in the next election.
       Hearer: Oh yes, I know who *it* is.

    b. Speaker: The rumour that a woman committed the murder shocked another woman.
       Hearer: Oh yes, I know who *it* is.

(20) *Sentential subjects*
    a. Speaker: Somebody's robbing the bank yesterday was seen by somebody else across the street.
       Hearer: Oh yes, I know who *it* was.

    b. Speaker: That some employee embezzled a million dollars is known by somebody else in the bank.
       Hearer: Oh yes, I know who *it* is.

In (19)–(20), it is grammatically possible for the italicized pronouns to refer to either of the two NPs in the previous sentences. However, the most natural interpretation of these pronouns is that they refer to the NPs occurring in the dominant clauses of the previous sentences. That is, in order for these responses to be pragmatically appropriate or cohesive with the previous discourse, the NP of S1 forming the referential link with S2 must be an NP from a dominant clause in S1. The fact that the pronouns are interpreted as referring to the NP of the dominant clauses is further evidence for the revised condition stated in (18).

2.2.3 Semantic connectors

Referential linking is one means by which cohesive discourse can result. According to Reinhart, sentences that are not referentially linked can still be cohesive if they are connected by semantic sentence connectors. An example of a sequence containing sentences that are not referentially linked but are cohesive is provided below:

(21) The first man landed on the moon. At the very same moment, a young boy died in Alabama.

(Reinhart 1980: 176)

Notice that the lack of referential linking in this passage is repaired by the semantic connector, *at the very same moment*, yielding cohesive discourse. As with referential linking, it is not the mere occurrence of a semantic connector that will produce cohesion. In fact, a similar restriction to that formulated in (18) also holds for the semantic connector condition for cohesion.

Consider the passages (22) and (23) below:

(22) The antibiotic which was discovered by Sir Alexander Fleming caused a great disturbance in the medical community. In addition, chaos resulted in universities across the country.

(23) The antibiotic which was discovered by Sir Alexander Fleming caused a great disturbance in the medical community. *In addition, a new species of germ was discovered.

Passage (23) is incohesive relative to (22). In passage (23), notice that the semantic connector, *in addition*, connects the second sentence to the semantic content of a non-dominant clause of the first sentence, the discovery by Sir Alexander Fleming. By contrast, in (22) the second sentence is connected to the content of a dominant clause of the preceding sentence, the occurrence of a great disturbance. The pragmatic inappropriateness of (23) relative to (22) demonstrates a restriction on the distribution of semantic connectors: semantic connectors must connect propositions that are contained within dominant clauses of adjacent or near-adjacent sentences in order for cohesive discourse to result.

The revised condition for referential linking exhibited in (18), along with the restriction on semantic connectors outlined above, can be generalized in the following way. Cohesive discourse results when some part of a sentence's dominant clause, that is, the main point of the sentence, is connected to succeeding sentences. When cohesive devices, whether they be referential links or semantic connectors, connect succeeding sentences to information that is not prominent (i.e. dominant) within the discourse, incohesive discourse results.

2.3 SUMMARY

I have suggested in this chapter that sequences of sentences conveyed from a single point of view be considered as belonging to the same discourse unit or episode. Given that discourse units are normally defined in terms of local coherence, this chapter has focused on the formal properties of explicitly coherent texts. (For the purposes of my investigation, I have distinguished between explicit and implicit coherence.) Cohesion is a necessary condition for explicit coherence and thus the last half of this chapter has been concerned with the precise formulation of conditions of cohesion.

I argue in the following two chapters that cohesion is one means by which RST interpretations are sustained beyond the level of a single sentence. That is, the interpretation of text fragments as being coherent in terms of the point of view conveyed is facilitated by the formal connectedness of sentences within particular discourse units. In Chapter 3, I look specifically at the cohesive devices of referential linking and semantic connector linking, demonstrating the way in which these devices contribute to the continuation of a particular discourse episode, i.e. a particular character's RST. In this way, we begin to understand the linguistic reflexes of point of view beyond the level of the sentence.

3

REFERENTIAL AND SEMANTIC CONNECTOR LINKING

3.0 INTRODUCTION

In this chapter, I argue that the cohesive devices of referential linking and semantic connector linking are means by which particular points of view (i.e. RST discourse units) are maintained across sentence boundaries. Chapter 1 described several syntactic constructions responsible for the emergence of a third person's point of view: direct discourse constructions within the broader context of indirect discourse and sentences containing parentheticals (SCPs). As suggested in Chapter 2, these syntactic constructions often signal the beginning of a discourse unit in which a character's point of view is represented. Consider the following example:

(1)   The sails flapped over their heads. The water chuckled and slapped the sides of the boat, which drowsed motionless in the sun. Now and then the sails rippled with a little breeze in them, but the ripple ran over them and ceased. The boat made no motion at all. Mr Ramsay sat in the middle of the boat. He would be impatient in a moment, *James thought*, and *Cam thought*, looking at their father, who sat in the middle of the boat between them (James steered; Cam sat alone in the bow) with his legs tightly curled. *He hated hanging about.*

(*To the Lighthouse*, 184)

The parentheticals, *James thought* and *Cam thought*, signal the beginning of an 'episode' whereby James's and Cam's point of view is represented. (Notice that the preceding sentences convey events from an objective point of view.) As part of the same discourse unit, the final sentence of (1) is also interpreted as James's and Cam's impressions of their father, in spite of the absence of any sentential markers of RST. The question that will be investigated in this chapter is how such an interpretation is facilitated by cohesion or the formal connectedness of sentences.

3.1 DOMINANCE AND SENTENCES CONTAINING PARENTHETICALS

Because SCPs often signal the beginning of new RST episodes (as in (1) above), I first examine the dominance possibilities of their clauses in order to establish their potential for creating cohesive discourse. Some representative examples of SCPs are provided below:

(2) a. She$_i$ knew all about *that*, said Mrs Ramsay$_i$.
(To the Lighthouse, 77)

b. She$_i$ had been reading fairy tales to James, she$_i$ said.
(To the Lighthouse, 79)

c. Yes, he did say disagreeable things, Mrs Ramsay admitted; . . .
(To the Lighthouse, 8)

d. Human relations were all like that, she thought. . . .
(To the Lighthouse, 107)

e. Where were her$_i$ paints, she$_i$ wondered.
(To the Lighthouse, 167)

In the remainder of this section, I show that the parenthetical clauses of SCPs are non-dominant. In this way, SCPs differ from their corresponding sentences with embedded-*that* clauses (e.g. *She said that she had been reading fairy tales to James*) as both clauses of the latter are potentially dominant as long as the embedded clauses are not islands (this was shown in Chapter 2). In other words, SCPs differ from their corresponding sentences with embedded-*that* clauses in that the clauses containing verbs of consciousness in SCPs are non-dominant. In section 3.1.1, I argue that the occurrence of root transformations in what I am calling the root-Ss[1] of SCPs shows that they are potentially dominant. In section 3.1.2, I show the results of the lie-test and the question-test, both of which get at the dominance possibilities of clauses, and argue that the results of these tests show the root-Ss of SCPs to be dominant and their parentheticals to be non-dominant, regardless of discourse context.

POINT OF VIEW

3.1.1 Root transformations

Emonds (1976) distinguishes between two large classes of transformations–structure-preserving and root transformations. Structure-preserving transformations produce structures that can also be generated by the phrase-structure rules; root transformations produce structures not generated by the phrase-structure rules. Emonds' hypothesis constrains the application of root transformations to matrix sentences, while structure-preserving transformations can apply to either matrix or embedded sentences.

Hooper and Thompson (1973), in a response to Emonds' structure-preserving hypothesis, argue that the distribution of root transformations is better explained in semantic rather than structural terms. More specifically, they state that root transformations apply only in sentences that are asserted.[2] They explain that the function of most root transformations is emphasis and that emphasis is inappropriate in clauses that are not asserted. For example, VP preposing, a root transformation, is acceptable in a complement sentence whose matrix verb is non-factive (i.e. the complement proposition is not presupposed but asserted):

(3)   Sally plans for Gary to marry her, and he vows that marry her he will.

In contrast, when VP preposing occurs in a complement sentence whose matrix verb is factive (i.e. the complement proposition is presupposed but not asserted), the result is ungrammatical for most speakers:

(4)   *Sally plans for Gary to marry her, and it bothers me that marry her he will.

The transformation of VP preposing functions to make the clause it appears in emphatic. Hooper and Thompson contend that it is inappropriate to emphasize elements of a sentence that are presupposed and whose content does not constitute the main point of a speaker's utterance. Thus, (3) is grammatical because the transformation applies in an asserted clause and (4) is ungrammatical because the transformation applies in a presupposed clause. For purposes of text analysis, we can use the occurrence of root transformations within a given clause as an indication that the particular clause is asserted.

The notions of assertion and dominance are closely related. Hooper and Thompson explain assertion as follows:

The assertion of a sentence is its core meaning or main proposition. In most cases the assertion of a declarative sentence is found in the main clause. The assertion of a sentence may be identified as that part which can be negated or questioned by the usual application of the processes of negation and interrogation. It is usually assumed that all assertions are speaker assertions. We will claim here, however, that some embedded statements have the characteristics of assertions, as can be seen when the tests of negation and questioning are strictly applied.

(Hooper and Thompson 1973: 473)

Recall that Erteschik-Shir and Lappin define dominance in a similar way, as the part of a sentence to which the speaker intends to direct the hearer's attention in uttering the sentence. The similarity between assertion and dominance is also evident in the operational tests used to identify asserted and dominant constituents within sentences. Hooper and Thompson claim that the assertion of a sentence is the part of a sentence that can be negated. Similarly, Erteschik-Shir and Lappin propose the lie-test as a means of determining which constituents are dominant. If the content of a clause can be denied and yield pragmatically appropriate results, then the clause in question is said to be dominant. Asserted constituents are those 'whose truth is in question or being discussed in the discourse context' (Hooper and Thompson 1973: 475). Thus, their truth can be appropriately denied by the lie-test, which makes them dominant constituents in Erteschik-Shir and Lappin's terms. Hooper and Thompson claim that both matrix and some embedded clauses have the potential of being asserted, just as Erteschik-Shir and Lappin claim that they both have the potential of being dominant.

As Hooper and Thompson note, root transformations are acceptable in certain complement sentences (i.e. those that are asserted or dominant). Some of these are exemplified below:

(5)   a. I exclaimed that never in my life had I seen such a crowd.
     b. I think that most embarrassing of all was falling off the stage.
     c. The scout reported that beyond the next hill stood a large fortress.

The following root transformations have applied in these sentences: negative constituent preposing in (5a), preposing around 'be' in (5b), and prepositional phrase preposing in (5c). Hooper and Thompson explain the application of these transformations, of course, in terms of the asserted nature of the complement sentences. All of the complements above are asserted. When the complement proposition is interpreted as the main assertion of a sentence, the matrix verb is used in its parenthetical sense and undergoes what Hooper and Thompson term a 'semantic reduction'. In this way, a sentence like (6a) (with the complement proposition as the main assertion) is synonymous with a sentence containing a parenthetical like (6b):

(6)   a. I think that most embarrassing of all was falling off the stage.
b. Most embarrassing of all was falling off the stage, I think.

We have seen in both Erteschik-Shir and Lappin's work and Hooper and Thompson's work that a sentence with an embedded-*that* clause (like 6a) has two possible asserted or dominant clauses. The realization of one or the other as dominant is dependent to some extent on discourse context. (Of course, in the case of (6a), the application of the root transformation indicates that the complement clause is asserted or dominant.) Sentences containing parentheticals differ from sentences with embedded-*that* clauses in that only one of their clauses (what I am calling the root-S) can be interpreted as dominant, regardless of discourse context. That the root-Ss of SCPs are dominant is demonstrated in the following sentences from Woolf's novels where root transformations have applied within the asserted sentences of the SCPs:

(7)   *Subject–aux inversion*
a. ... would her mother sanction their game, or condemn it, she wondered.
(*To the Lighthouse*, 134)
b. Had he blown his brains out, they asked, had he died the week before they were married. ...
(*To the Lighthouse*, 34)
c. ... could they tell her the way to Regent's Park Tube station – Maisie Johnson wanted to know.
(*Mrs Dalloway*, 30)

(8)   *Topicalization*
a. Such fools we are, she thought, crossing Victoria Street.
(*Mrs Dalloway*, 6)

b. Insoluble questions they were, it seemed to her, standing there. ...
   (To the Lighthouse, 12)
   c. And there is a dignity in people; a solitude; even between husband and wife a gulf; and that one must respect, thought Clarissa. ...
   (Mrs Dalloway, 132)
   d. Yes, but then these she had put in with her own hands, said Mrs Ramsay.
   (To the Lighthouse, 77)

(9) *Right dislocation*
   a. They were both out of things, Mrs. Ramsay had been thinking, both Lily and Charles Tansley.
   (To the Lighthouse, 119)
   b. It is probably the Queen, thought Mrs. Dalloway, coming out of Mulberry's with her flowers: the Queen.
   (Mrs Dalloway, 19–20)

(10) *Adverb preposing*
   a. And here she was, she reflected, feeling life rather sinister again. ...
   (To the Lighthouse, 70)
   b. Away and away the aeroplane shot till it was nothing but a bright spark; ... thought Mr Bentley. ...
   (Mrs Dalloway, 32)

From this discussion, we can conclude that when verbs of speech or thought are used in their parenthetical sense either in SCPs or in sentences with embedded-*that* clauses, they are reduced in terms of semantic force and their accompanying clauses are interpreted as dominant. As far as SCPs are concerned, the fact that root transformations occur in the root-Ss of SCPs is evidence for this claim.

3.1.2 Parentheticals and the 'lie'-test

While the previous section shows that the root sentences of SCPs have the potential of receiving a dominant interpretation, no evidence has yet been provided that shows that these root clauses are obligatorily dominant, regardless of the discourse context in which they occur. In this section, I examine the dominance possibilities of the parentheticals of SCPs. Following Erteschik-Shir and Lappin, and Hooper and Thompson, I make use of the lie-test (denying the

POINT OF VIEW

truth of a clause's proposition) and the question-test (questioning the propositional content of some clause of a given sentence) in order to determine the possibility of a parenthetical clause being dominant. The results of these tests show that a parenthetical clause cannot receive a dominant interpretation. (The parentheticals should be read with non-final intonation to differentiate true SCPs from a sequence of two distinct Ss – e.g. Ortcutt was a spy. John said (so).)

(11) John said Ortcutt was a spy.
 a. But that's a lie, he didn't.
 b. But that's a lie, he wasn't.

(12) Ortcutt was a spy, John said.
 a. *But that's a lie, he didn't.
 b. But that's a lie, he wasn't.

In example (11), both the matrix and complement clause can be denied. In example (12), on the other hand, the root-S can be denied but the parenthetical cannot.

(13) Mrs Ramsay said that he could have been a great philosopher.
 a. But that's a lie, she didn't.
 b. But that's a lie, he couldn't have.

(14) He could have been a great philosopher, said Mrs Ramsay.
 a. *But that's a lie, she didn't.
 b. But that's a lie, he couldn't have.

(15) Fred said that Jim refused to participate.
 a. But that's a lie, he didn't (say that).
 b. But that's a lie, he didn't (refuse).

(16) Jim refused to participate, Fred said.
 a. *But that's a lie, he didn't (say that).
 b. But that's a lie, he didn't (refuse).

In (13) and (15), both the matrix and complement clauses can be denied. In (14) and (16), it seems inappropriate to deny the truth of the parenthetical. It is, however, appropriate to deny the truth of the root-S in (13) and (15).

Similar results can be observed with the question-test. The question-test determines the appropriateness of a clause within a sentence providing the answer to a given question. Constituents that can appropriately provide an answer to a given question are considered to be dominant, i.e. contain the main content of the sentence.

(17) What tone of voice did Fred use in response to your question?
   a. He said emphatically that he would not get involved.
   b. *He would not get involved, he said emphatically.

(18) Who responded to your question about joining the committee?
   a. Fred said that he would join.
   b. *He would join, Fred said.

(19) How did Mary break the news to you?
   a. She announced very calmly that she had won the scholarship.
   b. *She had won the scholarship, she announced very calmly.

(20) Who told you about Mary's success?
   a. Joan told me that she had won the scholarship.
   b. *She had won the scholarship, Joan told me.

In (17) and (19), the questions concern the way in which a particular person performed a speech event. Notice that the questions are answered appropriately only when the answer is contained within the matrix clause of speech. When the matrix clause, which contains the answer to the question, occurs in its postposed position (as in 17b and 19b), the response does not provide an appropriate answer to the question. Similarly, in (18) and (20), the answer to the question is contained within the matrix clause of speech. In this case, it is the subject of the main verb that provides the answer to the question. Again, the SCP versions of the response are inappropriate as answers to the original questions. Notice that in all of these examples the information necessary to answer the questions is always contained somewhere within the responses. Because the necessary information is contained in parentheticals in the (b) sentences but the parentheticals are non-dominant, the SCP responses are inappropriate. The parenthetical clauses do not contain information that the speaker is attempting to direct the hearer's attention to in uttering the SCP and, therefore, cannot appropriately contain the answer to a given question.

On the other hand, it is quite appropriate for the root-S of an SCP to contain information that provides the answer to a given question.

(21) Who won the scholarship?
   a. Fred said that Mary won the scholarship.
   b. Mary won the scholarship, Fred said.

(21a) shows the appropriateness of the complement clause of an embedded-*that* clause containing information that provides the answer to the question. (21b) shows the appropriateness of the root-S of an SCP containing such information. Thus, both of these clauses are potentially dominant.

What the lie-test and the question-test demonstrate, then, is the obligatory dominance of root-Ss in SCPs and the obligatory non-dominance of the parenthetical clauses in these sentences.

3.2 COHESION AND SENTENCES CONTAINING PARENTHETICALS

As dominance is crucial to conditions of cohesion (this was demonstrated in Chapter 2), SCPs restrict the type of sentence that can follow them cohesively in a text. Given the non-dominance of parentheticals and the revised condition for referential linking and semantic connector linking formulated in Chapter 2, the prediction is that cohesive discourse will *not* result if the initial NP of a referential link comes from a parenthetical or if a semantic connector links material to the proposition of a parenthetical clause.

3.2.1 Referential linking, SCPs, and represented speech and thought

That this prediction is correct with respect to referential linking is demonstrated below. In these examples, cohesive discourse results when a sentence following an SCP in discourse has as its topic a referent from the root-S of that SCP (i.e. the SCP's dominant clause). Consider the following passage from Woolf's *To the Lighthouse*:

(22) . . . till Lily thought, How childlike, how absurd she was, sitting up there with all her beauty opened again in her, talking about the skins of vegetables. She was irresistible. Always she got her own way in the end, Lily thought.
(*To the Lighthouse*, 116)

The passage is Lily Briscoe's RST as indicated by the initial parenthetical, *Lily thought*; Lily Briscoe is observing Mrs Ramsay, contemplating her power. The final sentence of the passage is also an SCP, *Always she got her own way in the end, Lily thought.* In (23) below, I have provided two sentences that are both referentially linked to the final sentence of the preceding passage to the extent that they both contain NPs that are coreferential with NPs of the SCP (S1). The question is whether both sentences could follow directly after the SCP of the passage and create cohesive discourse:

(23) a. Even Lily succumbed to her.
b. *Even she managed to control Lily.

Notice that in both sentences (23a) and (23b) there is a topic of S2 which is referentially controlled by a referent in S1. In (23a), this topic is *her* (denoting Mrs Ramsay) and, in (23b), this topic is *Lily* (as is indicated by their non-occurrence with *even*). Thus, both sentences have a topic that is referentially linked to an NP of the preceding SCP. This fulfills Reinhart's condition on the second NP participating in the referential link being topic. However, (23b) is pragmatically odd (relative to (23a) at least) as a continuation of the passage in (22). We can attribute this lack of cohesion or pragmatic inappropriateness, in the one case, and cohesion or pragmatic appropriateness, in the other case, only to the dominance/non-dominance of the clauses within the SCP containing the relevant NPs. When the NP of S1, referentially controlling the topic of S2, occurs in the root-S of the SCP (the dominant clause), the sentences are cohesive. Conversely, when the NP of S1, referentially controlling the topic of S2, occurs in the parenthetical clause of the SCP (the non-dominant clause), the sentences are incohesive.

This is further evidence, then, for the revised condition for cohesion formulated in Chapter 2. Additionally, it suggests that cohesive discourse in RST depends, in part, on treating some aspect of a character's speech or thought as the topic of succeeding discourse. The interpretation of passage (22) as represented from Lily's point of view, is facilitated by the fact that all of the sentences are about Mrs Ramsay.[3] More specifically, the fact that sentences with no sentence-internal properties of RST such as *There was something frightening about her* and *She was irresistible* are interpreted as Lily's impressions of Mrs Ramsay (and not the narrator's) is the result of these sentences being formally connected to an SCP, which indicates explicitly that Lily is the source-consciousness. Put differently, referential linking contributes to an interpretation whereby Lily's point of view spans across sentences that have no explicit markers of RST.

The SCPs below, accompanied by referentially linked sentences that could potentially follow the SCPs in discourse, demonstrate the same phenomenon illustrated in (22) and (23). When the NP of S1, referentially controlling the topic of S2, occurs in the SCP's non-dominant clause (i.e. the parenthetical), the result is incohesive. When the NP of S1, referentially controlling the topic of S2, occurs in the SCP's dominant clause, the result is cohesive.

(24)   Odious little man, thought Mrs Ramsay, why go on saying that?
(To the Lighthouse, 18)
   a. Even she disliked him now.
   b. *Even he was disliked by her now.

(25)   His beauty was so great, she said. . . .
(To the Lighthouse, 76)
   a. Even she was overwhelmed by it.
   b. *Even it overwhelmed her.

(26)   Her father was dying there, Mrs Ramsay knew.
(To the Lighthouse, 33)
   a. Even she couldn't help him.
   b. *She couldn't help even him.

(27)   Her shoes were excellent, he observed.
(To the Lighthouse, 22)
   a. Even he couldn't have made them.
   b. *Even they couldn't have been made by him.
   c. *He couldn't have made even them.
   d. They couldn't have been made even by him.

With sentences that follow SCPs, then, the topic must be coreferential with an NP of the root-S if cohesive (explicitly coherent) discourse is to result. In less technical terms, what this means is that a sentence following an SCP must be about the part of the SCP to which the speaker is attempting to direct the hearer's attention, i.e. the content of the root-S. In these texts, the root-Ss of SCPs almost always designate the substance of a character's speech or thought.

In the remainder of this section, I argue that the cohesion that results from referential linking is one means by which an RST interpretation is sustained over sentences and, in particular, over sentences that do not themselves contain syntactic markers of RST. That is, referential linking has the effect of signalling the continuation of an RST episode. Recall that we are interested in accounting for the fact that certain sentences, unmarked syntactically as RST, sometimes reflect a character's viewpoint (RST) and at other times reflect the objective viewpoint of

REFERENTIAL AND SEMANTIC CONNECTOR LINKING

a narrator (narration). As syntactic features alone are not adequate in accounting for these differing interpretations, it seems necessary to examine these sentences in relation to the context in which they occur in order to explain their interpretation.

Consider the following examples:

(28) Minta$_i$, Andrew observed, was rather a good walker. *She$_i$ wore more sensible clothes than most women. She$_i$ wore very short skirts and black knickerbockers. She$_i$ would jump straight into a stream and flounder across.*
(*To the Lighthouse*, 86)

(29) Mr Ramsay sat in the middle of the boat. He$_i$ would be impatient in a moment, James thought, and Cam thought, looking at their father, who sat in the middle of the boat between them (James steered; Cam sat alone in the bow) with his legs tightly curled. *He$_i$ hated hanging about.*
(*To the Lighthouse*, 184)

(30) ... till Lily thought, How childlike, how absurd she$_i$ was, sitting up there with all her beauty opened again in her, talking about the skins of vegetables. *There was something frightening about her$_i$. She$_i$ was irresistible.* Always she got her own way in the end, Lily thought.
(*To the Lighthouse*, 116)

(31) How did she$_i$ manage these things in the depths of the country? he asked her. *She$_i$ was a wonderful woman.*
(*To the Lighthouse*, 116)

(32) Her father$_i$ was dying there, Mrs Ramsay knew. *He$_i$ was leaving them fatherless.*
(*To the Lighthouse*, 33)

(33) Strife, divisions, difference of opinion, prejudices twisted into the very fibre of being, oh that they$_i$ should begin so early, Mrs Ramsay deplored. They$_i$ were so critical, her children. *They$_i$ talked such nonsense.*
(*To the Lighthouse*, 11)

(34) Minta Doyle$_i$ and Paul Rayley$_j$ had not come back then. That could only mean, Mrs Ramsay thought, one thing. *She$_i$ must accept him$_j$ or she must refuse him.*
(*To the Lighthouse*, 64)

(35) Yet, thought Mrs Ramsay, comparing her with Minta, ... of the two Lily$_i$ at forty will be better. *There was in Lily$_i$ a thread of something....*
(*To the Lighthouse*, 120)

(36) Nothing could make her happy without him$_i$! Nothing! *He$_i$ was selfish. So men are. For he$_i$ was not ill. Dr Holmes said that there was nothing the matter with him$_i$.*
(*Mrs Dalloway*, 27)

(37) When he$_i$ felt like that he went to the Music Hall, said Dr Holmes. *He$_i$ took a day off with his wife and played golf.*
(*Mrs Dalloway*, 100–1)

In each of the above examples (with the exception of (36)), an SCP is followed by a sentence or sentences (the italicized ones) that do not themselves contain features of RST but are referentially linked to sentences with such features. That is, the italicized sentences' topics are referentially controlled by an NP in a dominant clause of the preceding SCP.[4] This referential linking has the effect of sustaining an RST interpretation over more than a single sentence. For example, it is not the narrator or formal speaker of the text who thinks that Minta wears sensible clothes or views Mrs Ramsay as irresistible or thinks that Mrs Ramsay's children talk nonsense, but rather Andrew, Lily, and Mrs Ramsay, respectively.

In example (36), the italicized sentences are referentially linked not to an SCP but to expressive sentences that also identify linguistic material as representing the speech or thought of a character. Preceding these expressives in the text, there is an SCP that identifies them as reflecting the consciousness of the referent of *she*, Rezia.

What is important to notice about the italicized sentences above is that they contain none of the syntactic features that Banfield describes as formally identifying sentences of RST (expressives, root transformations, character-oriented deictics), yet they are interpreted as characters' perceptions and impressions of narrative events. In fact, given a strict interpretation of Banfield, she predicts that some of these sentences should be ambiguous between RST and narration. She states that 'for sentences with ... stative verbs in the simple past, an explicit NOW [character-oriented deictic word] is required to disambiguate them: otherwise in narrative they can *either* be interpreted as narration per se or as sentences containing a SELF at a moment of consciousness' (Banfield 1982: 157; my emphasis). Thus, Banfield's prediction about the stative verbs with simple past tenses in the above examples is that they are ambiguous with respect to RST vs narration because they do not contain character-oriented deictics to disambiguate them.[5] I think it would be clear to the most unsophisticated reader of literature that the italicized sentences above containing stative verbs in the simple past tense are not ambiguous between RST and narration. For example, the stative verb sentences such as *There was something frightening about her, She wore very short skirts and black knickerbockers, He was selfish* are not ambiguous in terms of point of view. In the contexts above, they are clearly the impressions of characters at the time of the narrated events. Identifying these kinds of sentences unambiguously as sentences of RST requires looking beyond the sentence to their discourse context. More specifically, identifying the formal connectedness of these sentences to sentences explicitly marked as RST accounts correctly for their interpretation as sentences of RST.

The following passage shows more conclusively the relationship between referential linking and the interpretation of sentences as RST:

(38) [a] She liked Charles Tansley, she [Mrs Ramsay] thought suddenly; she liked his laugh. [b] She liked him for being so angry with Paul and Minta. [c] She liked his awkwardness. [d] There was a lot in that young man after all. [e] And Lily, she thought, putting her napkin beside her plate, she always has some joke of her own. [f] One need never bother about Lily. [g] She waited. [h] She tucked her napkin under the edge of her plate. [i] Well, were they done now? [j] No. [k] That story had led to another story.

(*To the Lighthouse*, 126)

In (38), ambiguity arises owing to a tension between the discourse features of the passage and its semantic content. Sentence [e] is an SCP and sentence [f] is referentially linked to it. As a result of the referential linking, [f] is interpreted as part of Mrs Ramsay's RST, more specifically as an impression of Mrs Ramsay's regarding Lily. Because sentence [g] is also potentially cohesive (i.e. referentially linked) to sentence [e], it is also interpreted (at least, initially) as part of Mrs Ramsay's RST. That is, the *she* of *she waited* is interpreted as designating Lily and the predicate as Lily's habitual activity as perceived through the consciousness of Mrs Ramsay. Upon reading further, however, the semantic content of the passage belies this interpretation. Sentence [h] predicates the action of tucking a napkin under the edge of her plate to *she* and we know from the semantic content of a previous sentence in the passage that it is Mrs Ramsay who has put her napkin beside her plate. Sentences [i] and

[j] provide further support for this latter interpretation as they are expressives indicating that it is, indeed, Mrs Ramsay who is waiting. Of crucial importance here is the fact that there exists ambiguity at all. It is because of the potential referential link between *She waited* and previous RST discourse that the initial (but ultimately incorrect) reading arises. That this initial reading even exists provides evidence for my claims regarding the effect of referential linking on the continuation of RST discourse units.

3.2.2 Semantic connector linking, SCPs, and represented speech and thought

According to Reinhart (1980) (as stated in Chapter 2), sentences that are not referentially linked can still be cohesive if they are connected by sentence semantic connectors. Like the referential linking condition for cohesion, the semantic connector condition also depends on the dominant clause of a sentence being connected to succeeding discourse. With respect to SCPs, then, semantic connectors must connect propositions to the content of an SCP's root-S in order for cohesive discourse to result. The following examples demonstrate that this is, indeed, the case:

(39) That man, she thought, her anger rising in her, never gave; that man took.
 (To the Lighthouse, 170)

(40) a. She, *on the other hand*, would be forced to give.
 b. *Mrs Ramsay, *on the other hand*, was less harsh in her judgements of other people.

Sentence (39) is an SCP representing Lily's impressions of Mr Ramsay. In (40), I have provided two sentences, each of which is to be read as following (39) in discourse. Notice that (40b) is pragmatically odd (at least relative to (40a)) as a continuation of (39). Notice also that both sentences have a semantic connector, *on the other hand*, that relates their content to the content of the preceding SCP. The difference is that in (40a) the proposition is connected to the root-S of the SCP, while in (40b) it is connected to the parenthetical of the SCP. In (40a), Lily's own behaviour is contrasted with her perception of Mr Ramsay's behaviour. In (40b), Mrs Ramsay's judgements of other people are contrasted with Lily's thoughts regarding Mr Ramsay. The relative inappropriateness of (40b) as compared to (40a) is further evidence for the revised semantic

REFERENTIAL AND SEMANTIC CONNECTOR LINKING

connector condition formulated in Chapter 2. More specifically, it can be seen that cohesive discourse results in these texts when semantic connectors link succeeding material to the content of characters' represented speech and thought.

Semantic connector linking has a similar effect to referential linking in these texts; it functions to sustain an RST interpretation over sentences that do not themselves contain markers of RST. Consider the following examples:

(41) He was thinking of himself and the impression he was making, as she could tell by the sound of his voice, and his emphasis and his uneasiness. Success would be good for him. *At any rate they were off again.* Now she need not listen.
(To the Lighthouse, 122–3)

(42) He thought, women are always like that; the vagueness of their minds is hopeless; it was a thing he had never been able to understand but so it was. It had been so with her – his wife. They could not keep anything clearly fixed in their minds. *But he had been wrong to be angry with her* [his daughter]; moreover, did he not rather like this vagueness in women? It was part of their extraordinary charm.
(To the Lighthouse, 190)

(43) Still, better poor Grizzle than Miss Kilman; . . . Better anything, she was inclined to say. But it might be only a phase, as Richard said, such as all girls go through. It might be falling in love. But why with Miss Kilman? who had been badly treated of course; one must make allowances for that, and Richard said she was very able, had a really historical mind. *Anyhow they were inseparable,* and Elizabeth, her own daughter, went to Communion; . . .
(Mrs Dalloway, 14)

In all of these examples, the italicized sentences are connected to preceding discourse by the semantic connector beginning each sentence. Because the preceding discourse is identified as RST by SCPs and/or other sentence-internal markers (e.g. root transformations, incomplete sentences), the sentences containing the semantic connectors receive the same interpretation in terms of point of view. For example, no syntactic feature of a sentence such as *But he had been wrong to be angry with her* of passage (42) identifies it as a character's judgement as opposed to the objective narrator's. Rather, it is the inter-sentential linking achieved by the semantic connector *but* that facilitates the RST interpretation.

3.3 DEMARCATION OF DISCOURSE UNITS

I have said that referential and semantic connector linking are discourse means by which RST discourse units are sustained beyond the level of a single sentence. As discourse units are normally marked for beginning and end in 'semantically conspicuous ways' (van Dijk and Kintsch 1983), a question that arises concerns the effect of discourse boundary markers on referential and semantic connector linking. In particular, do markers that have been independently identified as signalling episode boundaries influence the cohesive effect of referential and semantic connector linking?

Paragraph indentations in written discourse are a well-known signal of episode boundaries. Reinhart (1980), for example, considers the initial sentence of a paragraph to be exempt from her conditions on cohesion among sentences. This is presumably because paragraph breaks coincide with shifts in the topic of a discourse. From a reading perspective, Stark (1988) hypothesizes that paragraph boundaries create or signal discontinuities in texts, which may tell readers not to infer close semantic relations between sentences that occur across paragraph boundaries. Thus, while referential and semantic connector linking can signal the continuation of an RST interpretation, paragraph boundaries may mark the end of such units.

To confirm the effect of paragraph breaks on the interpretation of sentences as RST, consider the following example:

(44) But this question of love (she [Mrs Dalloway] thought, putting her coat away), this falling in love with women. Take Sally Seton; her relation in the old days with Sally Seton. Had not that, after all, been love?

She sat on the floor – that was her first impression of Sally – she sat on the floor with her arms round her knees, smoking a cigarette.

(*Mrs Dalloway*, 37)

Like example (38) above, this passage exhibits ambiguity as a result of tension between the discourse features of the passage and its semantic content. The second paragraph boundary in this passage serves to delimit a discourse unit, seemingly signalling the end of the RST episode of the previous paragraph (i.e. Mrs Dalloway's observations of Sally Seton). Thus, initially it seems that *She sat on the floor* refers to a narrative present activity of Mrs Dalloway's. Even though this sentence is potentially referentially linked to sentences in the preceding paragraph, the paragraph boundary has the effect (at least, initially) of favouring a non-RST reading. Reading further into the second paragraph, it becomes clear, on the basis of semantic content, that this paragraph is a continuation of Mrs Dalloway's musings about Sally Seton. *She*, therefore, designates Sally Seton, and *sat on the floor* her behaviour at a point prior to the narrative present. Again, the very existence of this ambiguity provides evidence for the role of discourse markers in the interpretation of RST. It is, *inter alia*, the paragraph boundary that demarcates a discourse unit and leads the reader to the initial non-RST interpretation of the second paragraph.

3.4 SUMMARY

In this chapter, I have demonstrated that the inter-sentential devices of referential and semantic connector linking facilitate the interpretation of characters' points of view within sentences that contain no internal markings of RST. In less formal terms, what this means is that a character's point of view will be maintained across sentence boundaries if succeeding discourse is linked to the content of a character's speech and thought. At the same time, I have tried to show the effect of discourse segmentation (i.e. paragraph boundaries) on the interpretation of RST discourse units. While referential and semantic connector linking are discourse means by which RST units are sustained within a discourse, episode boundary markers may interrupt this linking and potentially alter the interpretation of succeeding discourse, in terms of point of view.

4

TEMPORAL LINKING

4.0 INTRODUCTION

In this chapter, I show that temporal linking is another discourse means by which particular points of view (i.e. RST episodes) are maintained across sentence boundaries. I first outline a framework developed for the interpretation of temporal expressions in English (Smith 1978, 1980, 1981). I then stipulate a condition for cohesion called temporal linking, and provide semantic evidence to show the relationship between point of view and temporal linking. Finally, I discuss the inadequacy of previous treatments of RST with respect to sequence of tense.

In the previous chapter, I showed referential and semantic connector linking to be means by which an RST interpretation is sustained over sentences that do not themselves contain markers of RST. Below, I provide examples of sentences that are neither syntactically marked as RST nor linked by a referential tie or semantic connector to explicitly marked sentences of RST. The sentences in question are, however, interpreted as representing a character's point of view.

(1) That man, she [Lily] thought, her anger rising in her, never gave; that man took. She, on the other hand, would be forced to give. *Mrs Ramsay had given.* Giving, giving, giving, she had died – and had left all this. Really, she was angry with Mrs Ramsay.

(*To the Lighthouse*, 170)

(2) And off they went together walking right across the room, giving each other little pats, as if they hadn't met for a long time, Ellie Henderson thought, watching them

go, certain she knew that man's face. A tall man, middle aged, rather fine eyes, dark, wearing spectacles, with a look of John Burrows. *Edith would be sure to know.*

(*Mrs Dalloway*, 188)

In example (1), all of the sentences are interpreted as being the represented thought of the SCP's parenthetical subject, *she* (Lily Briscoe); in example (2), all of the sentences are interpreted as being the represented thought of Ellie Henderson. While the italicized sentences are neither referentially linked to the SCPs that begin these passages nor linked by a semantic connector, they are coherent with other sentences in the passage in terms of point of view. In the remainder of this chapter, I formulate a condition for cohesion called temporal linking, which will account for the interpretation of sentences such as the italicized ones above as RST.

4.1 TEMPORAL LINKING AS A COHESIVE DEVICE

Neither Reinhart (1980) nor Halliday and Hasan (1976) discuss the relationship between verb tense agreement and cohesion. Gutwinski (1976), in his study of cohesive devices in the prose of Henry James and Ernest Hemingway, states that sequence of tense can function as a cohesive device. This claim is, however, never illustrated or analysed in any detail. Reinhart (1983), while not explicitly dealing with cohesion, hints at the cohesive function of tense agreement. She notes that certain sentences of RST do not contain parentheticals indicating explicitly the source of the represented speech or thought. Her analysis of these sentences has parentheticals occurring in the deep structure but deleted in surface structure. Reinhart justifies her abstract analysis by claiming that it is the tense agreement within these sentences (the tenses of the root-Ss agreeing with their 'deleted' parentheticals) that indicates that a parenthetical exists underlyingly. If we look at this phenomenon in the discourse domain rather than the sentential, the tense agreement can be viewed as a discourse device for connecting parenthetical-less sentences to SCPs. I refer to this tense agreement phenomenon as temporal linking because of its connecting or cohesive function.

Previous treatments of texts such as the ones under investigation (Dry 1975; Fillmore 1981; Banfield 1982) identify back-shifted tenses as one of the hallmarks of RST. In particular, Dry and Banfield both comment on the occurrence of back-shifted modals (*will, can, shall*) in independent sentences within RST. The fact that *would, could,* and *should* in such sentences do not denote their usual meanings of conditionality, possibility, and obligation, respectively, is an indication that they are back-shifted from their original present tense forms. (*Would,* for example, in the italicized sentence of (2), does not represent conditionality but rather is a back-shifted form of the future, *will.*) In addition, Banfield notes that the simple past tense is back-shifted to the past perfect tense in RST. She provides the following example:

(3) 'We walked in the Park ... ' She stopped. They had walked in the Park.
(Banfield 1982: 103, from V. Woolf, *The Years*)

Banfield points out that what is simple past in the direct quotation is back-shifted to the past perfect in RST (the final sentence is the RST of the referent of *she*). Notice that the italicized sentences in (1) and (2) above exemplify the back-shifted simple past tense (*Mrs Ramsay had given*) and the back-shifted future (*Edith would be sure to know*). While Banfield and Dry are certainly correct in their observations regarding back-shifted tenses in RST, it is not clear from their comments how the presence or absence of back-shifting is identifiable solely on the basis of a sentence's internal properties. For example, the sentence below from *Mrs Dalloway* is an independent sentence in the past perfect tense:

(4) The face itself *had been seen* only once by three people for a few seconds.
(*Mrs Dalloway*, 19)

Yet from its context (see section 4.4.2), it is obvious that example (4) is not a back-shifted sentence of RST. My account of temporal linking distinguishes between the different interpretations available to a tense such as the past perfect. Specifically, by considering the discourse context in which these tenses occur, their interpretation as RST or narration can be accounted for.

4.2 INTERPRETATION OF TEMPORAL EXPRESSIONS

This section will outline a framework developed for the interpretation of temporal expressions in English by Smith (1978, 1980, 1981). In particular, the interpretive principles by which complement clauses receive temporal interpretations will be outlined. These principles will be extended in order to account for the interpretation of independent sentences that depend on other sentences within a discourse for their complete temporal interpretation.

Following Reichenbach (1947), Smith (1978, 1980, 1981) argues that the interpretation of temporal expressions requires three notions of time – speech time (ST), reference time (RT), and event time (ET). ST refers to the time at which a particular sentence is uttered, RT refers to the time indicated by a sentence, and ET refers to the time at which the sentence's event or state occurred. RT is oriented to ST. That is, if RT is simultaneous with ST, then RT indicates present time; if RT precedes ST, then RT indicates past time; if RT follows ST, RT indicates future time. ET may be, but is not necessarily, simultaneous with RT. In (5) below, ET and RT are the same and occur before ST:

(5)   John graduated last week.

Last week represents the RT, the time indicated by the sentence, and the time of graduation (ET) is the same as RT. The tense of the sentence is past, indicating that the ET and RT occurred before the time of the speech act (ST). In (6), all three of the times are different:

(6)   John had already completed his paper last week.

The RT is last week, the ET is an unspecified time prior to last week, and the ST occurs after both RT and ET.

The RT of a particular sentence is established by a combination of tense and time adverbials. The combination of present tense and a time adverbial explicitly indicating the present, for example, establishes an RT that is simultaneous with ST, as exemplified in (7):

(7)   He is playing now.

A combination of present tense and an explicitly future time adverbial, however, establishes an RT that is posterior to ST, as in (8):

(8)   Chris is working tomorrow.

And a combination of past tense and an explicitly past time adverbial establishes an RT that is anterior to ST, as in (9):

(9)   John ran away yesterday.

Some adverbials do not explicitly indicate past, present, or future, and Smith refers to these as unanchored or flexible. An unanchored adverbial, such as *on Tuesday* or *in January*, can indicate an RT that is anterior or posterior to ST. Example (10) shows *on Tuesday* indicating an RT posterior to ST, while (11) shows the same adverbial indicating an RT anterior to ST.

(10) John leaves on Tuesday.

(11) John left on Tuesday.

Thus, it is the combination of the tense and the time adverbial that establishes the RT of a particular sentence.

Sentences with tense alone are often incomplete semantically from the point of view of temporal interpretation. They are, in general, interpreted by means of information from the context in which they occur. Smith (1978) provides the following example. The sentence, *Albert is playing tennis*, may be interpreted in more than one way, depending on the context in which it occurs:

(12) a. Something unusual is scheduled for tomorrow:
      b. Albert is playing tennis.

(13) a. We can't discuss the problem now:
      b. Albert is playing tennis.

In (12), the RT is future time, posterior to ST, while in (13) the RT is present time, simultaneous with ST. The particular temporal interpretation is based on the discourse surrounding the sentence in question, as the sentence itself has no time adverbial.

In attempting to account for temporal interpretation across sentences, Smith (1980) introduces the notion of *extended temporal structures*. For example, the (b) sentences above do not establish a temporal interpretation on their own but depend on the (a) sentences for their complete interpretation. These sequences are what Smith terms extended temporal structures. Adopting a military metaphor, she characterizes the relationship between the (a) and (b) sentences above as a captor/captive one. She then distinguishes among different kinds of captive sentences: those that demand capture, those that are available for capture, and those that are protected from capture. Sentences with no time adverbials (such as the (b) sentences in (12) and (13) above) or with dependent adverbials (e.g. *previously, later*) demand capture; they require temporal information from another sentence of the surrounding discourse in order to establish RT. Sentences with unanchored or flexible time adverbials (e.g. *on Tuesday*) are available for capture; they can be captured but will anchor to ST if they lack temporal information from their context. And sentences with deictic adverbials (e.g. *now, tomorrow*) are protected from capture. Because they are oriented to ST, they cannot be anchored to times established in other sentences.

As Smith notes, exceptions to this generalization regarding sentences with deictic adverbials appear frequently in the kinds of texts under investigation here. That is, deictics in these texts are not oriented to ST (the speech time of the presumed narration) and thus their sentences do not establish a temporal interpretation on their own. In Smith's terms, such sentences demand capture; they require an RT to which their deictics can be re-anchored.

Captive sentences (those that demand or are available for capture) in extended temporal structures establish their RTs through 'sharing'. Sharing is a type of temporal dependency relationship that can exist between matrix sentences and their complement clauses or between independent sentences. Smith (1978) describes the sharing principle in her discussion of matrix and complement clauses; it involves a time in a matrix sentence functioning as the RT for its complement. Consider the interpretation of sentence (14):

(14) They told us yesterday that Tom had arrived three days earlier.

The complement sentence has a combination of tense and time adverbial that does not establish RT. Notice that, if it occurred on its own, it would not specify an RT from which the ET could be computed. However, when this sentence occurs as a complement clause of a matrix sentence that does establish RT, the complement clause is interpretable. We can say about (14) that Tom arrived three days prior to yesterday. Thus, we see that the RT of the matrix sentence is serving as the RT of the complement sentence. This is what Smith refers to as sharing; the complement clause shares the RT of the matrix clause. The fact that the temporal expression in the complement clause is interpretable at all indicates that it is getting its RT from elsewhere. In (14), the matrix sentence is the only possible source of this RT. As regards the temporal interpretation of independent sentences that are incomplete semantically, Smith speculates that an extended sharing principle is necessary. Such a principle would stipulate that sentences that are incomplete semantically require a neighbouring sentence with the same tense in order for their temporal interpretation to be complete. The RT of the neighbouring sentence would serve as the RT of the incomplete sentence. The neighbouring sentence (i.e. the captor) would serve the same function as the matrix sentence in (14) to the extent that it would contribute to the temporal interpretation of a sentence that is incomplete semantically.

4.3 TEMPORAL INTERPRETATION OF SENTENCES OF RST

Smith's sharing principle can be used to account for the temporal interpretation of many sentences of RST. It will first be demonstrated that this principle is necessary to account for the temporal interpretation of the root-Ss of SCPs. These clauses are like the complement clause of (14) to the extent that they depend on their parentheticals for the establishment of their RTs.

It is a characteristic of narratives that they create a timeline – a narrative present – in which fictional events occur. A reader of such a narrative is aware of a narrative past, present, and future with events of the narrative present serving to move time forward in the fictional world. This timeline is often created without an explicit indication of its precise temporal reference. For example, the following passage from *Mrs Dalloway* indicates only that events in the narrative present are taking place in the month of June:

(15) It was June. The King and Queen were at the Palace. And everywhere, though it was still so early, there was a beating, a stirring of galloping ponies, tapping of cricket bats. . . .

(Mrs Dalloway, 7)

Even though there is little information in this passage regarding the precise time at which events take place, it is clear that the 'beating', 'stirring', and 'tapping' take place in the narrative present on the main time axis of the narrative and that this narrative present occurs during the month of June. Aristar and Dry (1982) maintain that, in conventional past tense narratives, a timeline event is one whose ET coincides with RT, where RT is anterior to the narrator's presumed ST.[1] That is, the RT of a conventional past tense narrative is the narrative present and this narrative present is represented by verbs in the simple past tense (events whose ET coincides with RT). As can be seen in passage (15), sentences in the simple past tense with no time adverbials are interpreted as being part of the narrative present. Therefore, within the context of a narrative, where little temporal information regarding the narrative present is provided, sentences in the simple past tense receive a *complete* temporal interpretation. Their RT is established as being the narrative present despite the paucity of adverbials indicating the precise time of the narrative present.

While there is often no precise information given in *To the Lighthouse* and *Mrs Dalloway* about the time of the narrative present, deictic adverbs are oriented to this narrative present. As indicated above, deictic adverbials in these texts are not anchored to ST and, thus, must be re-anchored to a time established in surrounding sentences. Smith (1980) provides the following example:

(16) a. John said something surprising at noon.
     b. Mary had resigned an hour ago.

The deictic adverbial *an hour ago*, which would normally be anchored to ST, is anchored here to the time established in (16a). That is, Mary resigned at 11:00 a.m. Likewise, in the following examples from Woolf (SCPs), the deictics are anchored not to ST but to the RT established by the predicates of the SCP's parentheticals:

(17) a. It was terribly dangerous work for a one-armed man, she exclaimed, to stand on top of a ladder like that – his left arm had been cut off in a reaping machine *two years ago.*
        (*To the Lighthouse*, 14)

   b. And it was still going on, Mrs Ramsay mused, gliding like a ghost among the chairs and tables of that drawing room on the bank of the Thames where she had been so very, very cold *twenty years ago*;
        (*To the Lighthouse*, 101)

   c. She was trying to get these tiresome stockings finished to send to Sorley's little boy *tomorrow*, said Mrs Ramsay.
        (*To the Lighthouse*, 37)

   d. There wasn't the slightest possible chance that they could go to the Lighthouse *tomorrow*, Mr Ramsay snapped out irascibly.
        (*To the Lighthouse*, 37)

In (17a), *two years ago* represents a time not two years before the time of the telling of *To the Lighthouse* but rather two years before the point in the narrative present at which Mrs Ramsay exclaims. Similarly, in (17b) *twenty years ago* represents a time twenty years prior to Mrs Ramsay's musings. And in (17c) and (17d) *tomorrow* represents the day after the day in the narrative present on which Mrs Ramsay's and Mr Ramsay's speech acts take place.

In Smith's terms, we can say that the sharing principle applies and that the RTs of the SCPs' parentheticals serve as the RTs for the SCPs' root-Ss. In (17a–d), the parentheticals denote events that occur in the narrative present. While these parentheticals do not establish as specific an RT as a sentence like (16a) does, it is clear that the root-Ss of the SCPs share the RT of their parentheticals as they are clearly anchored to the narrative present.

An extended version of the sharing principle is necessary to account for independent sentences of RST that are not syntactically connected to parentheticals but whose deictic adverbials are oriented to the RT of the narrative present. The difference between the examples in (17) and those in (18) below, then, is that in (18) the sentences containing the deictic adverbials are not the root-Ss of SCPs, but rather syntactically independent sentences.

(18)   a. All this bother about a brooch really didn't do at all, Andrew thought. . . . The tide was coming in fast. The sea would cover the place where they had sat *in a minute*.

(*To the Lighthouse*, 89)

      b. Where were her paints, she [Lily Briscoe] wondered? Her paints, yes. She had left them in the hall *last night*.
(*To the Lighthouse*, 167–8)

      c. She had said that *last night* looking out of the window with tears in her eyes. 'The mountains are so beautiful'. Her father was dying there, Mrs Ramsay knew.
(*To the Lighthouse*, 33)

Notice that, in all three examples above, the deictic adverbials are oriented to the narrative present rather than to ST. In (18a), *in a minute* indicates a time posterior to Andrew's thoughts, not a time posterior to ST. In (18b) and (18c), *last night* refers to the night before the day on which Lily Briscoe and Mrs Ramsay have these thoughts. These deictics are re-anchored to the RT of the text, the narrative present. The similarity between the examples in (17) and

(18) suggests that, in the case of (18), it is the parentheticals in neighbouring sentences designating events of the narrative present that provide the RT for the independent sentences. In the same way that the root-Ss of (17) depend semantically on the parentheticals of their SCPs, so the independent sentences of (18) depend on the parentheticals of neighbouring SCPs for their RT.

When considering the question of how certain independent sentences of RST get interpreted as such, I contend that this sharing relationship plays a role. The temporal relationship that exists between the independent sentences of (18) and their neighbouring parentheticals results in the independent sentences being interpreted as if they were complement sentences, in some sense. While not syntactically connected to the parentheticals, these independent sentences depend on the parentheticals for their temporal interpretation and hence can be viewed as the semantic 'complements' of these parentheticals. Because they are dependent on neighbouring parentheticals in the same way that root-Ss of SCPs are dependent on these same parentheticals (in terms of temporal interpretation), their point of view interpretation is the same. I claim that these independent sentences are *temporally linked* to their neighbouring parentheticals (while not syntactically linked to them) and that their interpretation as RST derives from this linking.

Up to this point, we have examined only independent sentences that have explicit temporal expressions requiring an RT. We have not yet examined independent sentences with no temporal expressions. Recall the italicized sentences of (1) and (2), repeated below for the reader's convenience.

(1)   That man, she [Lily] thought, her anger rising in her, never gave; that man took. She, on the other hand, would be forced to give. *Mrs Ramsay had given. Giving, giving, giving, she had died* – *and had left all this. Really, she was angry with Mrs Ramsay.*

(To the Lighthouse, 170)

(2)   And off they went together walking right across the room, giving each other little pats, as if they hadn't met for a long time, Ellie Henderson thought, watching them go, certain she knew that man's face. A tall man, middle aged, rather fine eyes, dark, wearing spectacles, with a look of John Burrows. *Edith would be sure to know.*

(Mrs Dalloway, 188)

The italicized sentences are not linked by a referential tie or by a semantic connector to previous discourse, yet they are interpreted as part of the same RST unit. What can be noticed about the italicized sentences of (1) and (2) is their similarity to the independent sentences of (18). While they do not contain deictic adverbials as the sentences of (18) do, they do indicate a time that requires further information from the context for its full interpretation. The italicized sentence in (1), with its past tense of the auxiliary *have*, does not establish an RT on its own. It is like the sentence *Ross had left on Tuesday*, in that no anchor or reference time is provided for the ET indicated in the sentence. Like the sentences of (17) and (18), the italicized sentence of (1) has the narrative present as its RT. (Its ET is anterior to this RT.) And, like the sentences of (17) and (18), it is the RT of a parenthetical (*she thought*) to which the italicized sentence of (1) is anchored. Again, because the sentence itself has no clause with which it can share an RT, it must find a neighbouring sentence to fulfil this function (a parenthetical, in this case).

The extended sharing principle is also necessary to account for the interpretation of the italicized sentence of (2). The predicate, *would know*, indicates a time that is posterior to some other time. (The modal *would* does not here express conditionality or habituality.) It is clear that this predicate is anchored to the RT of the narrative present as the designated event is understood as occurring posterior to Ellie Henderson's speculations regarding the identity of the unknown man. The parenthetical, *Ellie Henderson thought*, provides this RT. The italicized sentences of (1) and (2) depend for their temporal interpretation on preceding parentheticals in the same way that the root-Ss below depend on the parentheticals of their SCPs.

(19) a. Mrs Ramsay had given, she thought.
b. Edith would be sure to know, Ellie Henderson thought.

And it is this cross-sentential semantic dependence (what I term temporal linking) that accounts, in part, for the particular RST interpretations of the independent sentences of (1) and (2).

4.3.1 Semantic evidence

As a way of demonstrating that the independent sentences discussed in the previous section are, in fact, interpreted as RST, I will, in this section, present semantic evidence to that effect. Fillmore (1981) notes the absence of certain semantic material in RST, namely linguistic material that reflects information unknown to the character whose consciousness is being represented or linguistic material semantically inconsistent with what is known to the character. The following SCP would be odd within RST because the evaluative adjective *sweet* is semantically inconsistent with the proposition expressed in the root-S:

(20) #Yes, she disliked that sweet man immensely, Lily said.

Because the root-S reflects Lily's (and only Lily's) point of view, the contradictory information within this clause makes the sentence semantically anomalous.[2] In the same way, example (21) is semantically deviant because of the existence of contradictory propositions in a clause representing Lily's point of view:

(21) #Yes, she disliked him immensely although he was actually very sweet, Lily thought.

When such propositions or evaluative adjectives occur in RST and do represent information that the character has access to or information consistent with what is known to the character, then the epistemic qualifications are attributed to the character whose consciousness is being represented. For example, in the following passage the word *perhaps* is interpreted as representing the judgement of *her*, the character whose consciousness orients this passage:

(22) And it struck her, this was tragedy – not palls, dust, and the shroud; but children coerced, their spirits subdued. James was sixteen, Cam seventeen, *perhaps*.
(*To the Lighthouse*, 169)

I have inserted the word *probably* into the next passage, yielding similar results. Because it is semantically consistent with the character's knowledge and contained within RST, it is interpreted as the male character's judgement regarding the female character.

(23) . . . so he turned deliberately in his chair and looked out of the window and said, all in a jerk, very rudely, it would be too rough for her tomorrow. She would *probably* [my insertion] be sick.
(*To the Lighthouse*, 100)

In (20) and (21), the semantic deviance results from contradictory information being contained within a sentence attributed to the consciousness of one character. In (22) and (23), the linguistic material in question is not inconsistent with a character's knowledge or inaccessible to the character. Its occurrence within an RST unit causes it to be interpreted as a character's evaluation or judgement.

It can be noticed that there are other evaluative adverbials within passage (23), *all in a jerk* and *very rudely*. These adverbials are not attributed to the character whose speech is represented in this passage. Rather, they are interpreted as objective descriptions of the way in which the character's speech act is performed; thus, in our terms, they represent the narrator's perspective on the character's speech act. They are interpreted in this way because they are not contained within the root-S of the parenthetical. We can see, then, that no semantic deviance results if information unknown or inaccessible to a character is not contained within that character's RST but is contained within the narration of the text.

In the following section, I demonstrate how the interpretation of evaluative adjectives and adverbials and epistemic qualifications can differ, depending on the temporal linking that exists between an independent sentence and a previous sentence explicitly marked as RST. In other words, I will use the fact that a particular evaluative is interpreted as reflecting a character's perspective as evidence that the sentence is one of RST. I will use the fact that a particular evaluative is interpreted as reflecting the narrator's perspective as evidence that the sentence is one of narration. In addition, I will use the semantic deviance of a sentence containing linguistic material unknown to characters or contradictory with characters' knowledge as evidence that the sentence is one of RST.

4.3.2 Temporal linking and the interpretation of evaluative expressions

In (23) above, the SCP, . . . *and said,* . . . *it would be too rough for her tomorrow*, requires the sharing principle in order for the root-S to receive a temporal interpretation. The combination of past tense and future adverbial does not establish an RT; the RT of the root-S is oriented to the RT of the parenthetical, the narrative present. The final sentence of the passage, *She would probably be sick*, has a similar relationship to the parenthetical in that it is also interpreted as being posterior to the RT of the parenthetical. While not containing an explicit deictic adverbial requiring an RT, the final sentence of the passage contains an unanchored tense and thus also requires the RT of a neighbouring sentence. As a result of this semantic dependence, the independent sentence is linked to the preceding parenthetical, and its lexical item, *probably*, is attributed to the consciousness of the parenthetical subject.[3]

Consider passage (24) below:

(24) [a]. . .James kept dreading the moment when he [his father] would look up and speak sharply to him about something or other. [b]Why were they lagging about here? he would demand, or something quite unreasonable like that. [c]And if he does, James thought, then I shall take a knife and strike him to the heart.

(*To the Lighthouse*, 208)

Sentence (24)[b] in the above passage is an SCP but it does not denote a speech act that occurs in the narrative present. As stated previously, a timeline event in a conventional past tense narrative is one whose ET coincides with RT where the RT is past with respect to the narrator's presumed speech tme. Events represented by the simple past tense will generally be interpreted as timeline events and thus receive a complete temporal interpretation in spite of the absence of precise adverbials. Sentence (23)[b] is incomplete semantically because it contains the future modal, *will*, in its past tense form *would*. Further information from the context is necessary to complete the temporal interpretation of *he would demand*, as the RT to which the future modal is posterior is not established in the sentence itself. Sentence (24)[b] can be said to be oriented to the RT of the narrative present and, in particular, to the past tense predicate of *James kept dreading*. In this way, the interpretation of sentence (24)[b] as being posterior to the RT of the narrative present can be accounted for. Again, it is the semantic dependence of sentence (24)[b] on a predicate designating James's mental state that results in its interpretation as part of James's RST. This reading can be confirmed by inserting an evaluative adverb into the sentence:

(25) Why were they lagging about here? he would *probably* demand.

If (25) is read within the context of the original passage, the *probably* can only be interpreted as a judgement of James's. Notice how the interpretation of the passage would be altered if the father's speech act were represented by the simple past tense:

(26) [a]. . .James kept dreading the moment when he would look up and speak sharply to him about something or

other. [b]Why were they lagging about here? he demanded all in a flap.

Sentence (26)[b] is not as easily interpreted as a perception or observation of James's. (See Chapter 5 for a discussion of the representation of narrative present events in RST.) By contrast, (24)[b] is unambiguously a sentence of RST, reflecting James's point of view.

These different interpretations are explained by the presence or absence of temporal linking. Because the parenthetical of (26)[b] occurs in the simple past tense, it is interpreted as a timeline event. Timeline events do not require further information from the context for their temporal interpretation. No extended sharing principle is necessary; hence, this sentence is not temporally linked or connected, in the sense that I am using this term, with any other sentence in the discourse. In particular, it is not linked to a root-S of an SCP by virtue of its semantic dependence on a parenthetical and is not interpreted, in terms of point of view, like the root-S of an SCP. Sentence (24)[b], on the other hand, is semantically dependent on the sentence *James kept dreading* and is, therefore, interpreted as one of James's dreaded speculations about the future.

Other passages further illustrate the effect of temporal linking:

(27)   She [Lily Briscoe] would paint that picture now. Where were her paints, she wondered? Her paints, yes. She had left them in the hall last night. She would start at once. She got up quickly, before Mr Ramsay returned.
      She fetched herself a chair. She pitched her easel *with her precise, old-maidish movements* on the edge of the lawn, not too close to Mr Carmichael, but close enough for his protection.

(*To the Lighthouse*, 167–8)

This passage begins as the RST of Lily Briscoe, but in the second paragraph becomes narration. The italicized expressions of the second paragraph clearly reflect a perspective that is distinct from Lily Briscoe's and must be attributed to a narrator, as this is linguistic material that cannot appropriately be attributed to a character. Notice its inappropriateness within the root-S of an SCP reflecting a character's point of view.

(28)   #She$_i$ would pitch her easel with her precise, old-maidish movements, Lily$_i$ thought.

The attributive adjectives describing the movements in (28) are not descriptions a character would have access to or information a character would appropriately provide about himself/herself.

Consider the inappropriateness of inserting this narration material into the RST at the beginning of the passage:

(29) She would paint that picture now. Where were her paints, she wondered? Her paints, yes. *She had left them in the hall last night with her precise, old-maidish movements.* She would start at once.

The italicized sentence in (29) is pragmatically inappropriate within this context because it is linked to other sentences of Lily's RST by virtue of temporal linking. Because the unanchored tense (*had left*) and deictic (*last night*) require an RT for their complete temporal interpretation, they are semantically dependent on the preceding parenthetical, *she wondered*. The pragmatic inappropriateness of the italicized sentence of (29) is certainly one piece of evidence for the effect of temporal linking on the interpretation of sentences as RST. When linguistic material that is semantically incompatible with a character's perspective is inserted within this sentence, it does not cease to be conveyed from Lily's point of view. Rather, the combination of temporal linking and the semantically incompatible linguistic material results in pragmatic inappropriateness.

If the sentence is transformed so that the verb represents an event on the main timeline of the narrative, the results are different. Consider passage (30) below:

(30) She would paint that picture now. Where were her paints, she wondered. Her paints, yes. *She left the hall with her precise, old-maidish movements and fetched herself a chair.*

Because the verbs of the final sentence are in the simple past tense representing events of the narrative present, they require no temporal information from the surrounding discourse for their interpretation. The interpretation of the italicized sentence as narration (and not RST) derives from its lack of semantic dependence on a parenthetical verb within the surrounding discourse. That its content is not attributed to a character's consciousness is demonstrated by the sentence's compatibility with linguistic material that is inappropriately attributed to a character in (29).[4]

This section, then, has demonstrated the pragmatic inappropriateness that results when sentences, temporally linked to explicitly marked sentences of RST, contain linguistic material incompatible with or inaccessible to a character's knowledge.

4.4 ANCHORING PREDICATES

Up to this point, I have said that temporal linking occurs when unanchored tenses and/or adverbials find their RTs in neighbouring sentences. One effect of this temporal linking is the sustaining of RST interpretations over sentences that do not themselves contain linguistic markers of RST. In this section, I demonstrate that temporal linking does not necessarily have this effect. That is, the interpretation of sentences containing unanchored tenses as RST (as opposed to narration) depends upon the nature of the predicate to which the unanchored tenses are linked.

4.4.1 Anchoring predicates and RST

Most of the examples provided in this chapter show unanchored tenses and adverbials receiving their RTs from the predicates of neighbouring parentheticals. And, in conjunction with this linking, the sentences in question are interpreted as the RST of the parenthetical subject. Further examples are provided below:

(31) One$_i$ of his uncles kept the light on some rock or other off the Scottish coast, he said. He had been there with him$_i$ in a storm.

(*To the Lighthouse*, 106)

(32) He wished Andrew$_i$ could be induced to work harder. He$_i$ would lose every chance of a scholarship if he didn't.

(*To the Lighthouse*, 78)

(33) She turned with severity upon Nancy. He$_i$ had not chased them, she said. He$_i$ had been asked.

(*To the Lighthouse*, 8)

(34) But he was not going to be made a fool of by women, so he turned deliberately in his chair and looked out of the window and said, all in a jerk, very rudely, it would be too rough for her$_i$ tomorrow. She$_i$ would be sick.

(*To the Lighthouse*, 100)

The final sentences of examples (31)–(34) contain unanchored tenses that find their RTs in the preceding parentheticals. (The parentheticals contain predicates that denote events of the narrative present.) In our terms, then, these sentences are both referentially and temporally linked to the preceding SCPs. Support for this claim comes from the unambiguous interpretation that these sentences receive; they very clearly represent the point of view of the preceding SCP's source consciousness.[5]

It is also possible, of course, for sentences containing unanchored tenses to be linked to SCPs solely by means of temporal linking. Consider the examples below:

(35) Sir William explained to her the state of the case. *He [Septimus] had threatened to kill himself.* There was no alternative. It was a question of law. He would lie in bed in a beautiful house in the country. The nurses were admirable. *Sir William would visit him once a week.*
(*Mrs Dalloway*, 107)

(36) She seemed to have shrivelled slightly, he thought. She looked a little skimpy, wispy; but not unattractive. He liked her. There had been some talk of her marrying William Bankes once, but nothing had come of it. His wife had been fond of her. *He had been a little out of temper too at breakfast.*
(*To the Lighthouse*, 171)

Like the italicized sentences of (1) and (2), the italicized sentences above derive their interpretation as RST from their semantic dependence on the predicates of the preceding SCP's parentheticals or, in the case of (35), the preceding sentence *Sir William explained to her the state of the case.*

While the predicates that provide the RT for unanchored tenses and adverbials in passages (31)–(36) are all verbs of communication or consciousness, we see below that this is not always the case. Predicates designating characters' perceptions as well as those denoting characters' physical activities can serve to establish the RTs for unanchored tenses.

(37) She looked at him thinking to find this shown in his face; *he would be looking magnificent* ... But not in the least! He was screwing his face up, he was scowling and frowning and flushing with anger.
(*To the Lighthouse*, 110)

(38) He loathed people eating when he had finished. She saw his anger fly like a pack of hounds into his eyes.... He

sat there scowling. He had said nothing, *he would have her observe*. Let her give him credit for that!

(*To the Lighthouse*, 110)

(39) Clarissa guessed; Clarissa knew of course; she had seen something white, magical, circular, in the footman's hand, a disc inscribed with a name, – the Queen's, the Prince of Wales', the Prime Minister's? – which, by force of its own lustre, burnt its way through . . . to blaze among candelabras, glittering stars, breasts stiff with oak leaves, . . . the gentlemen of England, that night in Buckingham palace. And Clarissa, too, gave a party. She stiffened a little; *so she would stand at the top of her stairs*.

(*Mrs Dalloway*, 20)

(40) Her evening dress hung in the cupboard. Clarissa, plunging her hand into the softness, gently, detached the green dress and carried it to the window. *She had torn it. Somebody had trod on the skirt. She had felt it give at the Embassy party at the top among the folds.* . . . *She would mend it.* . . . *She would wear it tonight. She would take her silks*, her scissors, her – what was it? – her thimble, of course. . . .

(*Mrs Dalloway*, 42–3)

(41) And Lucy, coming into the drawing room with her tray held out, put the giant candlesticks on the mantlepiece, the silver casket in the middle, turned the crystal dolphin towards the clock. *They would come; they would stand; they would talk* in the mincing tones which she could imitate, ladies and gentlemen. Of all, her mistress was loveliest. . . .

(*Mrs Dalloway*, 43)

In (37) and (38) above, the RTs for the unanchored tenses (italicized in the passages) are supplied by the sentences *She looked at him* and *He sat there scowling*, sentences whose predicates denote characters' perceptions and expressions. Providing RTs for the unanchored tenses of examples (39)–(41) are predicates denoting characters' actions: *She stiffened a little, Clarissa . . . detached the green dress and carried it to the window, And Lucy . . . put the giant candlesticks on the mantlepiece . . . turned the crystal dolphin towards the clock*.

TEMPORAL LINKING

What passages (37)–(41) have in common is their description of specific characters' states and/or actions represented by predicates whose RT is the narrative present. It is the unanchored tenses' semantic dependency on these particular kinds of predicates that is responsible for their sentences' interpretation as RST.

4.4.2 Anchoring Predicates and Narration

To demonstrate that the interpretation of the unanchored tenses of (37)–(41) as RST is indeed controlled by the nature of the anchoring predicate, one need only look at examples where a tense such as the past perfect is anchored to a different type of predicate:

(42) The motor car with its blinds drawn and an air of inscrutable reserve proceeded towards Piccadilly, still gazed at, still ruffling the faces on both sides of the street with the same dark breath of veneration whether for Queen, Prince, or Prime Minister nobody knew. The face itself *had been seen* only once by three people for a few seconds. Even the sex was now in dispute.
(*Mrs Dalloway*, 19)

(43) Yet rumours were at once in circulation from the middle of Bond Street to Oxford Street on one side, to Atkinson's scent shop on the other, passing invisibly, inaudibly, like a cloud, swift, veil-like upon hills, falling indeed with something of a cloud's sudden sobriety and stillness upon faces which a second before had been utterly disorderly. But now mystery *had brushed* them with her wing; they *had heard* the voice of authority; . . . But nobody knew whose face had been seen.
(*Mrs Dalloway*, 17)

Because the italicized tenses in both passages (the past perfect) express anteriority to some past time, they require further information from their context in order to receive a full temporal interpretation. (The RTs are not supplied by the sentences themselves.) In both passages, the RTs are found in neighbouring sentences with predicates in the simple past tense (*proceeded, were*). What is essential to notice about these examples is that the narrative present events from which the unanchored tenses receive their RT are not verbs of communication or consciousness, or verbs that designate a specific character's perceptions or physical activities. And, because the unanchored tenses of (42) and (43) are linked to narrative present states and events that are not predicated of specific characters, these unanchored tenses are not interpreted as back-shifted tenses of RST. That is, the italicized sentences are attributed not to the consciousness of a character but rather to an objective narrator. Hence, we see that the interpretation of sentences as RST is determined, in part, by their temporal linking to *particular kinds* of anchoring predicates. If a neighbouring predicate of communication or consciousness or perception provides the RT for unanchored tenses, then the sentences in question will be interpreted as a character's RST. On the other hand, if the predicate providing the RT for an unanchored tense is not of the kind described above, the sentences in question will not be interpreted as reflecting a character's point of view. Put differently, temporal linking will have the effect of maintaining RST interpretations cross-sententially only if unanchored tenses are linked to particular kinds of character-oriented predicates.

4.5 DEMARCATION OF DISCOURSE UNITS

The previous section showed that the particular type of predicate to which a semantically incomplete tense anchors has an influence on its interpretation as RST or narration. In this section, I examine the relationship between the demarcation of discourse units and the interpretation of unanchored tenses. Given the segmentation function of paragraph boundaries described in Chapter 3, the expectation is that the textual discontinuity resulting from paragraph indentations will affect the anchoring possibilities of semantically incomplete tenses and, thus, their interpretation as back-shifted tenses of RST. The following examples demonstrate that discourse structure, specifically the demarcation of discourse units, determines (to some extent) the predicates to which unanchored tenses will link:

(44) Clarissa guessed; Clarissa knew of course; she had seen something white, magical, circular, in the footman's hand, a disc inscribed with a name, – the Queen's, the Prince of Wales', the Prime Minister's? – which, by force of its own lustre, burnt its way through . . . to blaze among candelabras, glittering stars, breasts stiff with oak leaves, . . . the gentlemen of England, that night in Buckingham palace. And Clarissa, too, gave a party. She stiffened a little; so she would stand at the top of her stairs.

> *The car had gone*, but *it had left a slight ripple* which flowed through glove shops and hat shops and tailors' shops on both sides of Bond Street. For thirty seconds all heads were inclined the same way – to the window.
>
> (*Mrs Dalloway*, 20)

(45) And as if she had something she must share, yet could hardly leave her easel, so full her mind was of what she was thinking, of what she was seeing, Lily went past Mr Carmichael holding her brush to the edge of the lawn. Where was that boat now? Mr Ramsay? She wanted him.

> *Mr Ramsay had almost done reading.* One hand hovered over the page as if to be in readiness to turn it the very instant he had finished it. He sat there bareheaded with the wind blowing his hair about, extraordinarily exposed to everything. He looked very old.
>
> (*To the Lighthouse*, 230)

(46) He had been to Amsterdam, Mr Bankes was saying as he strolled across the lawn with Lily Briscoe. He had seen the Rembrandts. He had been to Madrid. Unfortunately, it was Good Friday and the Prado was shut. He had been to Rome. Had Miss Briscoe never been to Rome? . . .

> *She had been to Brussels; she had been to Paris*, but only for a flying visit to see an aunt who was ill. She had been to Dresden; there were masses of pictures she had not seen; however, Lily Briscoe reflected, perhaps it was better not to see pictures: they only made one hopelessly discontented with one's own work.
>
> (*To the Lighthouse*, 83)

Coinciding with the paragraph break (in (45) the paragraph boundary is also a chapter break) in each of these examples is a shift in point of view. Example (44) shifts from Clarissa Dalloway's vantage point to the narrator's; example (45) from Lily Briscoe's to the narrator's;[6] and example (46) from Mr Bankes' to Lily Briscoe's. While semantic content is certainly partly responsible for these shifts (for example, in the first paragraph of (46) Lily Briscoe is asked a question by Mr Bankes, and the second paragraph of (46) constitutes an answer to this question), the textual discontinuity created by paragraph boundaries also contributes to the changes. In particular, the fact that paragraph breaks separate past perfect tenses (italicized in the passages) from previous RST discourse results in these tenses not anchoring to *preceding* narrative present predicates. Even though, for example, the semantically incomplete sentence of (44), *so she would stand at the top of her stairs*, is linked to the preceding narrative present predicate (*She stiffened a little*), the succeeding semantically incomplete sentences (*The car had gone, it had left a slight ripple*) are not linked to this same predicate. I am suggesting that the paragraph boundary is, in part, responsible for the anchoring possibilities of these incomplete tenses and, in turn, for their interpretation as RST vs narration. Likewise, even though the sentences *He had been to Rome* and *She had been to Brussels* of passage (46) are only one sentence apart, they are not interpreted as reflecting the same character's point of view. I am claiming that it is the paragraph boundary, *inter alia*, that separates these two instances of unanchored tenses; this results in their anchoring to different narrative present predicates (i.e. *Mr Bankes was saying* vs *Lily Briscoe reflected*) and receiving different point of view interpretations. Thus, in order to account for the shifts in point of view in (44)–(46), I suggest that the segmentation created by paragraph boundaries influences the anchoring possibilities of past perfect tenses, which, in turn, influences their sentences' point of view interpretation.

4.6 SUMMARY

In this chapter, I have shown temporal linking to be another discourse means by which RST interpretations are sustained beyond the scope of a single sentence. As stated at the outset of this chapter, other linguistic descriptions of RST have identified 'back-shifted' tenses as one of its distinctive characteristics (Banfield 1982; Dry 1975). However, because these other accounts state only that RST is signalled by back-shifted tenses, they cannot distinguish between the different point of view interpretations that are available to a tense such as the past perfect. By considering the phenomena of 'back-shifted tenses' within a discourse framework, my account of temporal linking can distinguish between instances of unanchored tenses that are interpreted as RST as opposed to those that are interpreted as narration. Instances of both kinds occur in texts containing RST, and discriminating between them depends crucially upon discourse factors, not exclusively sentential factors.

5

ASPECT, COHERENCE, AND POINT OF VIEW

5.0 INTRODUCTION

The previous two chapters have shown the cross-sentential scope of RST interpretations to be facilitated by referential, semantic connector, and temporal linking. In this chapter, I argue that sentences containing progressive aspect, in certain discourse contexts, convey events from a character's vantage point. While these sentences may not be textually cohesive with discourse containing syntactically marked sentences of RST, they are interpreted as coherent with them in terms of point of view. In Reinhart's terms, then, the sentences under discussion are ones that are *implicitly* coherent (as opposed to explicitly coherent) with other sentences within a segment.

Consider the following example:

(1) But what an extraordinary night! She felt somehow very like him – the young man who had killed himself. She felt glad that he had done it; thrown it away while they went on living. *The clock was striking.*

(*Mrs Dalloway*, 206)

The italicized sentence above does not exhibit referential, semantic connector, or temporal linking with previous discourse, yet it is coherent with the rest of the passage in terms of the point of view represented. All of the sentences in (1) are interpreted as reflecting Mrs Dalloway's (the referent of *she*) thoughts and perceptions. Certainly, the coherence of the passage derives, in part, from its semantic content. Interpreting it as coherent requires viewing the final sentence of (1) as a perception of Mrs Dalloway's. And this is possible, in part, because the italicized sentence denotes an event that can plausibly occur in the narrative present and be witnessed by a character such as Mrs Dalloway. However, it is not only the appropriateness of the sentence's content that is responsible for its coherence with previous RST discourse. It is also, crucially, presented in the progressive (imperfective) aspect.

The crucial contribution made by aspect to the incohesive but coherent sentence can be demonstrated by comparing passages such as (2) and (3) in which the final sentence has been altered.

(2) But what an extraordinary night! She felt somehow very like him – the young man who had killed himself. She felt glad that he had done it; thrown it away while they went on living. *Seth was catching a fish.*

(3) But what an extraordinary night! She felt somehow very like him – the young man who had killed himself. She felt glad that he had done it; thrown it away while they went on living. *Seth caught a fish.*

In passage (2), the final sentence is much like the final sentence of (1) in that it is not referentially or temporally linked to previous discourse or linked by a semantic connector. It is interpreted in the same way as the final sentence of (1), as a character's response to an ongoing event in the narrative present. This coherent interpretation of (2) requires that Mrs Dalloway is thinking about the young man who committed suicide in an outside setting where another character is fishing. While perhaps not a likely setting for Mrs Dalloway's ruminations on suicide, I think this reading imposes itself on the passage upon reading the final sentence, owing to its progressive aspect.

Passage (3) is more difficult to interpret as coherent. Because the final sentence occurs in simple or perfective aspect, it is not interpreted as a character's response to some event of the narrative present and, therefore, its lack of cohesion is more difficult to resolve. What I argue in the sections that follow is that 'incohesive' sentences of the kind discussed above are interpreted as coherent (implicitly coherent, in Reinhart's terms) with previous RST only if they are appropriate in terms of content (i.e correspond to some event that the character could plausibly observe in the narrative present) and if they occur in progressive aspect.

ASPECT, COHERENCE, AND POINT OF VIEW

5.1 PAST PROGRESSIVE AND POINT OF VIEW

In certain discourse contexts, the past progressive is interpreted as describing events from a character's point of view, an interpretation that is not as readily available with the simple past in the same context. In (4) below, I provide a passage from *To the Lighthouse* followed by sentences that continue the passage in both the progressive (imperfective) and simple (perfective) aspect. (These sentences should each be read as a continuation of the passage in (4).)

(4) He'd disinherit her if she married him, said Mr Ramsay. He did not look at the flowers, which his wife was considering, but at a spot about a foot or so above them. There was no harm in him, he added, and was just about to say that anyhow he was the only young man in England who admired his – when he choked it back.

(*To the Lighthouse*, 77)

(5) a. She had arranged these flowers with her own hands, *she was saying*.
b. She had arranged these flowers with her own hands, *she said*.
c. *She was saying* that she had arranged these flowers with her own hands.
d. *She said* that she had arranged these flowers with her own hands.

Sentences (5a) and (5c) present the speech event of *she*, the character Mrs Ramsay, in the progressive aspect, whereas sentences (5b) and (5d) represent the same event in the simple aspect. Corresponding to this difference in aspect is a difference in the vantage point from which the sentences are conveyed. In (5a) and (5c), Mrs Ramsay's speech event is relayed through the consciousness of another character – Mr Ramsay (i.e. from Mr Ramsay's point of view). Sentences (5b) and (5d), on the other hand, do not allow this interpretation as readily. Rather, when represented in simple aspect, this speech event reflects a point of view distinct from any character (i.e. the narrator's objective point of view).

The following passages illustrate further the relationship between point of view and progressive aspect to the extent that the events denoted in the progressive aspect are attributed to the character whose point of view orients the events of the immediately preceding discourse.[1]

(6) . . . for she thought, looking at James who kept his eyes dispassionately on the sail, or glanced now and then for a second at the horizon, you're not exposed to it, to this pressure and division of feeling, this extraordinary temptation. *Her father was feeling in his pockets; in another second, he would have found his book.*
(*To the Lighthouse*, 192)

(7) Looking at his hand he thought that if he had been alone dinner would have been almost over now; he would have been free to work. Yes, he thought, it is a terrible waste of time. The children were dropping in still. *'I wish one of you would run up to Roger's room,' Mrs Ramsay was saying.*
(*To the Lighthouse*, 102)

(8) . . . he felt come over him the disagreeableness of life, sitting there, waiting. Perhaps the others were saying something interesting? What were they saying?
That the fishing season was bad; that the men were emigrating. They were talking about wages and unemployment. *The young man was abusing the government.*
(*To the Lighthouse*, 108)

(9) But she did not know what it was about Sir William; what exactly she disliked. Only Richard agreed with her, 'didn't like his taste, didn't like his smell.' But he was extraordinarily able. *They were talking about this bill. Some case Sir William was mentioning, lowering his voice.*
(*Mrs Dalloway*, 202)

All of the italicized sentences in (6)–(9) are 'incohesive' with previous discourse as they are neither referentially nor temporally linked to it and contain no explicit semantic connector linking them to previous discourse. However, the italicized sentences are interpreted as the RST of the character whose RST occurs in the immediately preceding discourse. In (6), for example, the italicized sentence is interpreted as an observation of Cam's, the character designated by *she* who orients the previous discourse. In (7), the italicized sentence is interpreted as perceptions of the referent of *he*. In (8), the italicized sentence is interpreted as a perception of the referent of *he* from the previous paragraph. And in (9), the italicized sentences are understood as perceptions of Mrs Dalloway, the referent of *she*. In part, the interpretation of these sentences as RST is related to the fact that their semantic content corresponds to events in the narrative present that could plausibly be observed or perceived by the character whose RST occurs in preceding sentences. In addition, the fact that these sentences occur in progressive aspect facilitates their interpretation as RST. Comparable sentences in simple (perfective) aspect would be more difficult – perhaps impossible – to interpret as part of the RST of characters.

5.1.1 Evaluative words

The insertion of evaluative words into passages analogous to (6)–(9) provides confirmation that simple and progressive aspect differ in their point of view interpretations. Recall that in Chapter 4 it was shown that certain evaluative words are attributed to different points of view depending on whether they occur in RST or narration in the text. In the following passage, for example, the word *perhaps* is attributed to the character denoted by the pronoun *he*:

(10)   ... he felt come over him the disagreeableness of life, sitting there, waiting. *Perhaps* the others were saying something interesting? What were they saying?
(*To the Lighthouse*, 108)

Passages (11) and (12) below are like (10) except that, in (12), the progressive aspect has been transformed to simple aspect.

(11)   ... he felt come over him the disagreeableness of life, sitting there, waiting. Mrs Ramsay *was probably saying* that she would call the maid.

(12)   ... he felt come over him the disagreeableness of life, sitting there, waiting. Mrs Ramsay *probably said* that she would call the maid.

In (11), as in (10), the evaluative word *probably* is attributed to the character designated by *he*. In (12), however, the sentence containing the evaluative word is pragmatically odd in a way that the comparable sentence of (11) is not. The deviance of (12) derives from the incompatibility of simple aspect, which does not generally denote narrative present events from a character's point of view, and the evaluative word *probably*, which can only be attributed to some character within the fictional world.² On the other hand, the compatibility of the progressive aspect with a character's evaluation in (11) is a further indication that the progressive, in certain contexts, invokes a third person's point of view.

Another example of a similar phenomenon is provided below. Into passage (6) above, I have inserted an adverbial phrase describing the way in which Mr Ramsay (Cam's father) feels in his pockets.

(13)   . . . for she thought, looking at James who kept his eyes dispassionately on the sail, or glanced now and then for a second at the horizon, you're not exposed to it, to this pressure and division of feeling, this extraordinary temptation. Her father was feeling in his pockets *all of a sudden*; in another second, he would have found his book.

In this passage, *all of a sudden* is interpreted as Cam's impression of the way in which her father performs the action of feeling in his pockets. If this sentence is transformed from the progressive aspect to the simple aspect, then *all of a sudden* is interpreted as a narrator's description of Mr Ramsay's action. (This sentence should be substituted for the final sentence of (13).)

(13a) All of a sudden, her father felt in his pockets and brought out a book.

Mrs Ramsay's speech event from passage (7) above can be transformed to simple aspect in the same way, and the interpretation of adverbial phrases will also change. In (14) below, the adverbial phrase modifying Mrs Ramsay's speech act (in progressive aspect) is attributed to William Bankes, the referent of *he*:

(14)   Looking at his hand he thought that if he had been alone dinner would have been almost over now; he would have been free to work. Yes, he thought, it is a terrible waste of time. 'I wish one of you would run up to Roger's room', Mrs Ramsay was saying *all of a sudden*.

On the other hand, if sentence (15), with the speech act represented in simple aspect, is substituted for the final sentence of (14), then the adverbial phrase is understood as the narrator's description of the speech event:

(15)   'I wish one of you would run up to Roger's room', Mrs Ramsay said all of a sudden.

ASPECT, COHERENCE, AND POINT OF VIEW

From the semantic evidence above, then, we can see that the interpretation of sentences in the progressive aspect in passages such as (6)–(9) is altered when their predicates are transformed to simple aspect. The difference is related to point of view: the progressive aspect results in the sentence being interpreted as the RST of the previously mentioned parenthetical subject, while the simple aspect results in the sentence being interpreted as the narrator's recounting of events.

5.2 PROGRESSIVE VS SIMPLE ASPECT

Following Smith (1983), I distinguish between situation aspect and viewpoint aspect. Aspect, in general, is defined by Smith as a semantic property of a sentence as opposed to a property of a situation. A speaker/writer, when presenting an actual situation, has considerable choice as to how to present it. Smith provides the following example: suppose Mary swims every day. This situation can be presented syntactically in different ways. Mary's act of swimming can be presented as an event in itself or as one in a series of swims. In addition, one can present a particular act of swimming as complete or ongoing. Situation aspect refers to the first of these realizations – whether the situation is presented as an event (achievement or accomplishment), state (activity or stative), habitual action, etc. Viewpoint aspect refers to the second of these realizations – whether an event is presented as a whole with no reference to its internal structure (complete) or whether some moment that is non-initial and non-final is referred to in the presentation of an event (ongoing).

Viewpoint aspect, in English, is signalled by particular morphemes: the auxiliary *be* and *ing* (progressive aspect) alternates with the simple verb form (simple aspect). According to Smith, 'simple aspect makes linguistic reference to endpoints and progressive aspect makes linguistic reference to a time that is not an endpoint' (Smith 1983: 482). These definitions are strongly reminiscent of Comrie's (1976) distinction between perfective and imperfective aspect. According to Comrie, the perfective aspect does not explicitly refer to the internal temporal constituency of a situation, whereas imperfective aspect explicitly refers to the internal temporal structure of a situation.

The reference or lack of reference to endpoints (initial and final) characteristic of the simple and progressive aspect, respectively, can be demonstrated by conjoining an event sentence (achievement or accomplishment)[3] with an assertion of continuation.

(16) a.# Fred climbed the mountain this morning and he may still be climbing it.
b. Fred was climbing the mountain this morning and he may still be climbing it.

The semantic anomaly of (16a) is due to the incompatibility of simple aspect, which indicates the event had ended (by referring to endpoints), with an assertion of the continuation of the event. (Sentence (16a) is interpretable only if the clauses refer to separate acts – i.e. Fred, having climbed the mountain this morning, may have returned to it later and begun climbing it again.) Example (16b), on the other hand, shows no semantic incompatibility as the progressive aspect does not refer to the endpoints of the event and, therefore, can be conjoined with an assertion of the event continuing.

In sequences of sentences, the simple and progressive aspect also have different interpretations. When achievement and accomplishment predicates occur in simple aspect, they describe events that take place after the time of the previous sentence's event. For example, the accomplishment predicate, *sit down*, is interpreted below as occurring later than the time of Fred's walking into the room:

(17) Fred walked into the room. He sat down on the couch.

Because simple aspect refers to endpoints, the inception of Fred's sitting down is referred to in the second sentence of (17). Thus, it is interpreted as occurring after the previous sentence's event. The progressive aspect, on the other hand, does not refer to endpoints and, thus, receives a different interpretation in discourse.

(18) Fred walked into the room. The janitor was sitting down on the couch.

In (18), the predicate, *was sitting down*, is interpreted as overlapping with the event denoted in the previous sentence. Because its inception is not explicitly referred to by the progressive aspect, it is interpreted as ongoing and, in part, contemporaneous with Fred's walking into the room.

We see, then, that the progressive aspect within a discourse has the effect of indicating that an event is in progress, i.e. that it has begun previous to the time in the discourse when it is presented. If the progressive aspect within a discourse indicates that an event is in progress and ongoing, then the event will often be interpreted as ongoing with respect to some other event. It can be seen in (18) that the janitor's sitting down is interpreted as occurring before and during Fred's walking into the room. In contrast, the simple aspect of the second sentence of (17) does not imply that its event is contemporaneous with another event. What is conveyed by this sentence is that the two events of (17) are sequential rather than simultaneous.

The interaction of the semantic properties of the progressive aspect (as outlined above) and the discourse context in which the progressive occurs is responsible for the point of view interpretations evident in passages such as (6)–(9). Within a discourse, the progressive aspect allows the events it denotes to overlap with events of the surrounding discourse. Thus, in passages (6)–(9) the events represented in progressive aspect are interpreted as ongoing in the narrative and as overlapping with previous events of the narrative. For example, in passage (6), Cam's father's feeling in his pockets is presented as an event that has begun before it is actually introduced into the narrative. This event is understood as being contemporaneous with the most recently mentioned event of the narrative present, *she thought*. In fact, in all four of the passages, the discourse immediately preceding the event represented in progressive aspect describes events denoting the thoughts or perceptions of characters: *she thought* in (6), *he thought* in (7), *he felt* in (8) and *she did not know* in (9). While these events do not necessarily belong to the previous sentence of the discourse, they are the most recently designated event of the narrative present (i.e on the narrative timeline). Thus, the events in the progressive aspect are interpreted as overlapping with these characters' thoughts and perceptions. I claim that it is precisely when events in progressive aspect overlap with predicates of communication or consciousness that they are interpreted as part of a character's RST.[4] The events described in progressive aspect are understood as a character's observations or perceptions (i.e. relayed through the consciousness of a character) because they are contemporaneous with that character's thought events. Represented in simple aspect, the predicates of the italicized sentences of (6)–(9) would denote non-overlapping events of the narrative present, events that would take place *after* the thought events of the preceding sentences. This lack of contemporaneity does not facilitate interpretations whereby a character thinks and *at the same time* observes or perceives an event of the narrative present.

This difference between the simple and progressive aspect helps to explain the different points of view evident in sentences (5a)–(5d) above. The progressive aspect in (5a) and (5c) means that the speech event it describes overlaps with previous events of the narrative present, that is, Mr Ramsay's represented speech and thought. This contemporaneity allows for an interpretation whereby Mrs Ramsay's speech event is relayed through the consciousness of Mr Ramsay. Rather than occurring *while* Mr Ramsay thinks, the speech event of (5b) and (5d) occurs after the events of the previous discourse. The speech event, *she said*, is therefore not attributed to Mr Ramsay's thoughts.

In a similar fashion, the fact that Cam's father's feeling in his pockets in (6) is presented as simultaneous with Cam's thinking contributes to the interpretation of the italicized sentence as part of Cam's RST. Likewise, in passage (7), what is presupposed by the progressive aspect is that Mrs Ramsay's speech act began prior to the particular point in the narrative present when it is introduced. Because the most recently mentioned event of the narrative present is *he thought*, Mrs Ramsay's speech event in the progressive aspect is interpreted as contemporaneous with William Bankes'(the referent of *he*) thoughts and perceptions about having dinner with the Ramsays. It is precisely because these events are presented in the progressive aspect and, therefore, interpreted as ongoing in the fictional world, that they are interpreted as observations/perceptions of William Bankes rather than as observations/perceptions of the narrator.

All the italicized sentences of (1), (2), (5a), (5c), and (6)–(9) meet the pragmatic condition for RST – they all represent events that could plausibly be observed/perceived by a character in the narrative present. What I am claiming is that there is a further condition for these types of sentences being interpreted as RST – a linguistic condition. It is the progressive aspect that facilitates an interpretation whereby these sentences are understood as coherent with previous discourse explicitly designating a character's represented speech and thought.

5.2.1 Textual juxtaposition of events

A question that arises from the preceding discussion is whether it is the mere textual juxtaposition of narrative present events with predicates of communication or consciousness that creates the point of view interpretations imputed to the progressive aspect. That is, in an example such as (7) above, is it the mere textual juxtaposition of the sentences *The children were dropping in still* and '*I wish one of you would run up to Roger's room,'* Mrs Ramsay was saying with William Bankes' RST that results in these sentences also being relayed from this character's point of view?

In the passage below, I provide examples of speech events presented in the simple aspect:

(19)   She supposed it was all right leaving him to his own devices, Mrs Ramsay said, wondering whether it was any use sending down bulbs; did they plant them? 'Oh, he has his dissertation to write', said Mr Ramsay. She knew all about *that*, said Mrs Ramsay. He talked of nothing else. It was about the influence of somebody upon something. 'Well, it's all he has to count on', said Mr Ramsay. 'Pray Heaven he won't fall in love with Prue,' said Mrs Ramsay. He'd disinherit her if she married him, said Mr Ramsay. He did not look at the flowers, which his wife was considering, but at a spot about a foot or so above them. There was no harm in him, he added, and was just about to say that anyhow he was the only young man in England who admired his – when he choked it back. He would not bother her again about his books. These flowers seemed creditable, Mr Ramsay said, lowering his gaze and noticing something red, something brown. Yes, but then these she had put in with her own hands, said Mrs Ramsay.

(*To the Lighthouse*, 77; emphasis Woolf's)

Whereas the speech event in the italicized sentence of passage (7), in the progressive aspect, is interpreted as Mrs Ramsay's speech event as perceived by William Bankes, in (19) the speech events, in the simple aspect, are interpreted as relayed by the objective narrator. On examining passage (19) more carefully, one can see that, in a sequence such as the one below, the simple aspect of *said Mrs Ramsay* represents the event as beginning *after* Mr Ramsay's speech event:

(20)   'Oh, he has his dissertation to write', said Mr Ramsay. She knew all about that, said Mrs Ramsay.

This interpretation holds because simple aspect makes explicit reference to the initial endpoint of the event. In other words, the simple aspect does not represent the event as ongoing in the narrative upon its mention but as beginning and ending upon its mention.

In general, every speech event of passage (19) is presented in simple aspect and, therefore, is interpreted as sequential rather than simultaneous with preceding and succeeding speech events.

It is important to notice that in (20), Mrs Ramsay's speech event follows in the text immediately after another SCP whose parenthetical subject is Mr Ramsay. This is similar to passage (7) to the extent that Mrs Ramsay's speech event in (7) also follows an SCP. (William Bankes is the subject of this parenthetical.) The fact that the two speech events (in (20) and (7)) differ in terms of point of view indicates that it is not the mere juxtaposition (or near juxtaposition) of two SCPs that results in the second being interpreted as RST and, in particular, as the RST of the previous parenthetical's subject. Rather, the interpretation of one speech event as narration and the other as RST correlates with the fact that simple aspect represents an event as having begun and ended upon its mention while progressive aspect represents an event as ongoing.

5.3 PROGRESSIVE IN OTHER CONTEXTS

In the previous section, I have suggested that the progressive describes events from a character's point of view when these events overlap with predicates denoting a character's speech and thought. Given the dependence of this point of view interpretation on local discourse context, one would not expect the progressive aspect always to designate events of RST. The following passages illustrate the way in which the interpretation of the progressive is altered according to discourse context:

(21) He had been to Amsterdam, *Mr Bankes was saying* as he strolled across the lawn with Lily Briscoe. He had seen the Rembrandts. He had been to Madrid.
(To the Lighthouse, 83)

(22) And then, as they stood in the hall taking yellow gloves from the bowl on the malachite table and *Hugh was offering* Miss Brush with quite unnecessary courtesy some discarded ticket or other compliment, which she loathed from the depths of her heart and blushed brick red, Richard turned to Lady Bruton, with his hat in his hand, and said,
'We shall see you at our party tonight?'. . .
(Mrs Dalloway, 123)

Passage (21) begins a chapter and, as a result, a break is created between it and previous discourse. This means that Mr Bankes' speech act overlaps with no previous event of the narrative and, in particular, with no predicate describing a character's speech or thought. (The first sentence of (21) indicates explicitly that the speech act overlaps with Mr Bankes' strolling across the lawn.) The speech act is not relayed through a character's consciousness in spite of its progressive aspect because of these facts about the local discourse context. Rather, the speech act is presented objectively, that is, from no subjective point of view within the text.

Passage (22) is similar to (21) in that the event denoted by the progressive aspect does not overlap with a character's speech or thought event. In fact, it is explicitly indicated in the passage that Hugh's offering Miss Brush some unnecessary courtesy is contemporaneous with Richard's turning to Lady Bruton. Furthermore, the fact that (22) marks the beginning of a paragraph means that previous events of the narrative are no longer salient or in focus. Given the nature of the local discourse context, the progressive aspect in (22), as in (21), is not interpreted as representing an event from a character's point of view.

The contribution of local discourse context to the interpretation of point of view is further evidenced if Mr Bankes' speech event of (21) is inserted into another context.

(24) Looking at her hand she thought that if she had been alone, dinner would have been almost over now; she would have been free to work. Yes, she thought; it is a terrible waste of time. He had been to Amsterdam, *Mr Bankes was saying*. He had seen the Rembrandts.

When Mr Bankes' speech act overlaps with a character's thought, as it does in (23), it is interpreted as reflecting that character's point of view. This particular interpretation can be explained only in terms of the discourse context of (23) as opposed to the discourse context of (21). Hence, it is the semantic properties of the progressive aspect combined with the nature of a predicate's local discourse context that determines a progressive predicate's point of view interpretation.

5.4 CONCLUSION

Banfield (1982) has also considered the role of aspect in texts characterized by RST. As discussed in Chapter 1, Banfield likens the simple past/past progressive alternation in English to the aorist/imparfait alternation in French. According to Banfield, these aspectual alternations correspond in both languages to narration/RST respectively. In other words, narration is represented or signalled by the simple past/aorist, and RST by the past progressive/imparfait. (Banfield claims that this is not true for stative verbs in English, which cannot appear in progressive aspect at all.) It has been demonstrated in Chapter 4 that the presence of a particular tense/aspect is not sufficient, in itself, to account for the interpretation of certain sentences as RST and other sentences as narration. It was shown that the past perfect tense is not always a 'back-shifted' tense of RST and that the interpretation of a sentence containing the past perfect tense as narration or RST is dependent on local discourse factors.

In the same way, the past progressive does not necessarily signal RST. When events represented in progressive aspect overlap with events of communication or consciousness, the event in question will be understood as a character's RST. This contemporaneity with a particular character's speech or thought facilitates the interpretation of a sentence in progressive aspect as being a perception/observation of the preceding parenthetical subject (providing, of course, that the content of the sentence corresponds to an event that can realistically be perceived by this character at the particular point in the narrative when it occurs). It is also, however, possible for an event represented by progressive aspect to be contemporaneous with some other event of the narrative present (i.e. not a character's speech or thought event). In passages (21) and (22), for example, the progressive does not represent events of RST. Banfield, of course, does not distinguish between these differing interpretations of the past progressive, dealing only with the progressive aspect as a marker of RST. In the framework adopted here, the interpretation of the past progressive depends, crucially, on its discourse context.

The RST sentences under discussion in this chapter are different from the RST sentences of previous chapters to the extent that they are not necessarily 'cohesive' with previous discourse explicitly marked as RST.[5] This is not to say, however, that their linguistic properties are not crucial to their point of view interpretation. Rather, I have argued that their coherence with previous RST discourse derives from the progressive aspect within a particular discourse context.

6

CONCLUSIONS

6.0 INTRODUCTION

This chapter summarizes the major points of the study by analysing several longer passages from *To the Lighthouse* and *Mrs Dalloway*. Having established the linguistic correlates of point of view above the level of the sentence, I then consider the function of these inter-sentential linguistic devices within Woolf's novels of 'revelation'.

6.1 SUMMARY: COHESION, COHERENCE, AND RST

A central aim of this book has been to make explicit the inter-sentential linguistic clues that readers use in identifying characters' points of view. The passage below demonstrates how referential linking contributes to this end:

(1) [a] Minta, Andrew observed, was rather a good walker. [b] She wore more sensible clothes than most women. [c] She wore very short skirts and black knickerbockers. [d] She would jump straight into a stream and flounder across. [e] He liked her rashness, but he saw that it would not do – she would kill herself in some idiotic way one of these days. [f] She seemed to be afraid of nothing – except bulls. [g] At the mere sight of a bull in a field she would throw up her arms and fly screaming, which was the very thing to enrage a bull of course. [h] But she did not mind owning up to it in the least; one must admit that. [i] She knew she was an awful coward about bulls, she said. [j] She thought she must have been tossed in her perambulator when she was a baby. [k] She didn't seem to mind what

she said or did. [l] Suddenly now she pitched down on the edge of the cliff and began to sing some song about

Damn your eyes, damn your eyes.

[m] They all had to join in and sing the chorus, and shout out together:

Damn your eyes, damn your eyes,

but it would be fatal to let the tide come in and cover up all the good hunting-grounds before they got on to the beach.

(*To the Lighthouse*, 86)

Sentence [a] is an SCP followed by sentences that are referentially linked to this SCP (either directly or by transitivity). By virtue of this cohesion, the content of these sentences is interpreted as Andrew's (the parenthetical subject of [a]) perceptions of Minta. The referential linking condition, then, has the effect of imputing sentences that are 'about' some aspect of the content of a previous parenthetical subject's speech or thought to that parenthetical subject, even though the sentences are not syntactically marked as RST. Sentences [i] and [j] of this passage are particularly noteworthy because they contain verbs of speech or thought (*she said, she thought*) in the simple past tense, which often, in these narratives, represent events of the narrative present that move time forward in the depicted world. In the context of this passage, however, the events represented by the verbs *said* and *thought* in sentences [i] and [j] are interpreted as an habitual event and stative, respectively. Notice that if these two sentences were considered out of this particular context, there would be no way of explaining their interpretation as non-narrative present events because the decontextualized sentences would allow – perhaps even favour – a main time axis interpretation. The fact that they are referentially linked to other sentences that explicitly identify Andrew as the source consciousness of the discourse unit determines, in part, their interpretation as Andrew's perceptions of Minta.

Sentence [l] of this passage contains predicates that, in other contexts, could also be interpreted as narrative present events conveyed from the perspective of an objective narrator (*pitched down* and *began*). However, the sentence is referentially linked to other sentences of Andrew's RST and contains a character-oriented deictic *now*. As Banfield and others have pointed out, deictics such as *here* and *now* in these texts are assigned from the point of view of a

CONCLUSIONS

character and hence invoke a character's perspective. The adverbial, *suddenly*, forces a non-habitual reading upon the events represented in this sentence. Unlike sentences [i] and [j], then, sentence [l] is understood as designating not Minta's habitual activities and states but rather her actions in the narrative present as conveyed through the consciousness of Andrew.

While passage (1) demonstrates the effect of referential linking on the interpretation of point of view, passage (2) illustrates other inter-sentential devices by which an RST interpretation is sustained across sentence boundaries.

(2) [a] She [Prue] kept looking at Minta, shyly, yet curiously, so that Mrs Ramsay looked from one to the other and said, speaking to Prue in her own mind, You will be as happy as she is one of these days. [b] You will be much happier, she added, because you are my daughter, she meant; her own daughter must be happier than other people's daughters. [c] But dinner was over. [d] It was time to go. [e] They were only playing with things on their plates. [f] She would wait until they had done laughing at some joke her husband was telling. [g] He was having a joke with Minta about a bet. [h] Then she would get up.
(*To the Lighthouse*, 126)

While coherent in terms of point of view (i.e. Mrs Ramsay's consciousness orients this passage), not all of the sentences are referentially linked to sentences where it is explicitly indicated that Mrs Ramsay is the source consciousness. Sentence [c], for example, is linked to previous discourse by the semantic connector *but*. Sentences [e] and [g] have predicates in the progressive aspect, indicating that the represented activities are ongoing with respect to Mrs Ramsay's thoughts.[1] As argued in Chapter 5, the progressive aspect facilitates an interpretation whereby these activities are understood as relayed through the consciousness of this character. And sentences [f] and [h] contain unanchored tenses, requiring an RT from a neighbouring narrative present predicate. It is the narrative present predicates of inner speech, *she added* and *she meant*, that supply the RT for these sentences with unanchored tenses. By virtue of this fact, sentences [f] and [h] are temporally linked (see Chapter 4) to the preceding SCPs and are interpreted, in terms of point of view, in the same way – as the RST of Mrs Ramsay.

What is crucial to notice about sentences [b]–[m] in passage (1) and sentences [c]–[g] in passage (2) is that the vast majority of them contain no sentence-internal linguistic clues to RST.[2] They are, however, interpreted as representing the thoughts and inner speech of the characters whose point of view explicitly orients previous discourse – Andrew and Mrs Ramsay. Thus, by identifying inter-sentential phenomena to explain the point of view interpretations available to these syntactically unmarked sentences of RST, this study provides a more descriptively adequate account of the relationship between linguistic form and point of view.

In contrast to the two passages presented above, the following passage from the opening chapter of *To the Lighthouse* contains linguistic material related solely from the perspective of the narrator. This passage demonstrates that the narrator, in these texts, can describe events and provide descriptions that are similar in their semantic content to the events and descriptions of RST exemplified in the passages above.

(3) To her son these words conveyed an extraordinary joy, as if it were settled the expedition were bound to take place, and the wonder to which he had looked forward, for years and years it seemed, was, after a night's darkness and a day's sail, within touch. Since he belonged, even at the age of six, to that great clan which cannot keep this feeling separate from that, but must let future prospects, with their joys and sorrows, cloud what is actually at hand, since to such people even in earliest childhood any turn in the wheel of sensation has the power to crystallize and transfix the moment upon which its gloom or radiance rests, James Ramsay, sitting on the floor cutting out pictures from the illustrated catalogue of the Army and Navy Stores endowed the picture of a refrigerator as his mother spoke with heavenly bliss.

(*To the Lighthouse*, 5)

The semantic content of this passage is very similar to the semantic content of many sentences of RST exemplified in the passages (1) and (2) above and elsewhere in this study. The sentences are descriptions of James Ramsay, which in other contexts could be attributed to some character in the fictional world. In the context of the passage above, however, they are interpreted as being conveyed from the perspective of the objective narrator of the text. This interpretation follows, of course, from the lack of cohesion or coherence between

CONCLUSIONS

these sentences and other explicitly marked sentences of RST. We see again, then, that discourse context is crucial to an adequate linguistic account of point of view.

6.2 SUMMARY: DEMARCATION OF RST UNITS

The linguistic features summarized above have the effect of sustaining RST interpretations beyond the domain of single sentences. In contrast to grammatical features that mark the continuation of these kinds of discourse episodes, van Dijk (1982) has identified linguistic devices that serve to delimit and demarcate discourse units. Among the grammatical 'signals' that may be expected for the beginning of episodes, van Dijk lists paragraph indentations in written discourse, time change markers, place change markers, change of perspective markers, etc. In the texts under investigation here, the demarcation of discourse units often results in a shift in point of view. That is, the effects of referential linking, semantic connector linking, and temporal linking described in the previous section may be altered if the linking occurs in conjunction with some segmentation marker. In the passages below, for example, referential linking exists between the sentences at the paragraph boundaries:

(4) 'No going to the Lighthouse tomorrow, Mrs Ramsay', he [Mr Tansley] said asserting himself. He liked her; he admired her; he still thought of the man in the drain-pipe looking up at her; but he felt it necessary to assert himself$_i$.

He$_i$ was really, Lily Briscoe thought, in spite of his eyes, but then look at his nose, look at his hands, the most uncharming human being she had ever met.

(*To the Lighthouse*, 99)

(5) He [Mr Tansley] felt extremely, even physically, uncomfortable. He wanted somebody to give him a chance of asserting himself. He wanted it so urgently that he fidgeted in his chair, looked at this person, then at that person, tried to break into their talk, opened his mouth and shut it again. They were talking about the fishing industry. Why did no one ask him his opinion? What did they know about the fishing industry?

Lily Briscoe knew all that. Sitting opposite him could she not see, as in an X-ray photograph, the ribs and thigh

bones of the young man's desire to impress himself. . . .
(To the Lighthouse, 104)

Because the second sentence involved in each referential link is one that expresses Lily Briscoe's thoughts and perceptions explicitly, the referential linking does not have the effect of sustaining Mr Tansley's (the referent of *he*) RST beyond the final sentence of each preceding paragraph. The combination of the paragraph indentations and explicit change of perspective markers (i.e. *Lily Briscoe thought* and *Lily Briscoe knew*) segments the discourse in each passage and creates a shift in point of view (in spite of the referential linking).

Other passages display shifts in point of view that are achieved less explicitly. One of the grammatical signals included among van Dijk's list of episode boundary markers is the reintroduction of 'old' (previously mentioned) individuals with full NPs instead of pronouns. In a detailed study of anaphora and discourse structure, Fox (1987) makes a similar claim. She argues that the occurrence of full NPs, where one would have expected pronouns, are often used to demarcate new narrative units. In these texts, it is not just the use of full NPs for known characters that can signal a shift in point of view. In addition, a change in the proper name used to designate a given character can suggest a shift in source consciousness. Consider the following passage:

(6) She said she loved Bach. So did Hutton. That was the bond between them, and Hutton (a very bad poet) felt that *Mrs Dalloway* was far the best of the great ladies who took an interest in art. It was odd how strict she was. About music she was purely impersonal. She was rather a prig. But how charming to look at! She made her house so nice, if it weren't for her Professors. *Clarissa* had half a mind to snatch him off and set him down at the piano in the back room. For he played divinely.
(Mrs Dalloway, 195)

Even though the sentence in (6) containing the proper name *Clarissa* is referentially linked to previous sentences that clearly reflect Hutton's impressions of Mrs Dalloway, it is interpreted as a perception of Clarissa Dalloway's. The change from *Mrs Dalloway* to *Clarissa* as a designation for this character is, in part, responsible for this shift in point of view. That is, by representing this character with a proper name *not* within Hutton's repertoire of proper names for Clarissa Dalloway, the end of Hutton's RST is signalled. And

CONCLUSIONS

again, this occurs in spite of the referential linking that exists between the second last sentence of the passage and previous discourse. Thus, we see that the segmentation created by episode boundary markers can signal a shift in point of view (i.e. mark the end of a particular RST interpretation) even if linking does occur.

6.3 FUNCTION OF RST INTER-SENTENTIAL DEVICES

In summarizing the textual means by which RST discourse units are maintained and delimited, it becomes evident that the linguistic manifestations of coherence (at the local level) within these texts include features not usually discussed in relation to cohesion and coherence. As stated in Chapter 2, Reinhart (1980) formulates two conditions for cohesion, one involving referential linking and the other, semantic connector linking. While Halliday and Hasan (1976) provide an extensive taxonomy of cohesive devices (reference, substitution, ellipsis, conjunction, and lexical cohesion), Reinhart argues that their six major categories can essentially be reduced to her two conditions for cohesion. For example, much of Halliday and Hasan's reference, substitution, and lexical cohesion can be subsumed under Reinhart's referential link condition. And their category of conjunction can likewise be subsumed under Reinhart's semantic connector condition.

In a detailed study of cohesive devices in the prose of Henry James and Ernest Hemingway, Gutwinski (1976), using Halliday and Hasan's taxonomy, concludes that the number of cohesive devices used over a given portion of text does not differ significantly for the two writers. What does differ, however, is the kind of cohesive devices used by James and Hemingway. James, according to Gutwinski, depends heavily on grammatical cohesion (anaphora) as opposed to lexical cohesion (lexical repetition), whereas Hemingway uses almost as many lexical cohesive devices as grammatical ones. What is crucial to notice about these results is that all of these cohesive devices are instances of referential links. In fact, cohesion by means of semantic connectors was found to be very rare in both writers' prose. Thus, in all of the texts on which Halliday and Hasan's, Reinhart's, and Gutwinski's work is based, referential linking seems to be the most common type of cohesive device.

Distinct about the kinds of texts under investigation here is the frequent use of other types of linguistic features in the establishment of local coherence – namely semantic connector linking, temporal linking, and the progressive aspect. If we compare a passage like (1) above, characterized by referential linking, to a passage like (2), which achieves its coherence primarily through semantic connector linking, temporal linking, and the progressive aspect, we see that one of the differences between the two passages is the frequent topic shifts in (2). The referentially linked passage in (1) does not exhibit frequent topic shifts; the entire passage concerns Minta, the character in Andrew's immediate purview.[3] By contrast, the unity of the passage in (2) is *not* derived by the repetition of the same referent. Mrs Ramsay's attention turns from the time, to her dinner guests, to her own future actions. In general, RST passages characterized by referential linking do not display the abrupt topic shifts that are evident in RST passages characterized by semantic connector linking, temporal linking, and predicates in progressive aspect. Consider the passages below:

(7)   Oh yes, Sally remembered; she had it still, a ruby ring which Marie Antoinette had given her great-grandfather. She never had a penny to her name in those days, and going to Bourton always meant some frightful pinch. But going to Bourton had meant so much to her – had kept her sane, she believed, so unhappy had she been at home. But that was all a thing of the past – all over now, she said. *And Mr Parry was dead*; and Miss Parry was still alive.
(*Mrs Dalloway*, 208)

(8)   And off they went together walking right across the room, giving each other little pats, as if they hadn't met for a long time, Ellie Henderson thought, watching them go, certain she knew that man's face. A tall man, middle aged, rather fine eyes, dark, wearing spectacles, with a look of John Burrows. *Edith would be sure to know*.
(*Mrs Dalloway*, 188)

(9)   All this bother about a brooch really didn't do at all, Andrew thought, as Paul told him to make a 'thorough search between this point and that'. *The tide was coming in fast*. The sea would cover the place where they had sat in a minute.
(*To the Lighthouse*, 89)

While all of the passages exhibit coherence, the italicized sentences are not coherent with previous discourse by means of the cohesive device of referential linking. For example, the italicized sentence of example

CONCLUSIONS

(7) is connected to previous discourse by a semantic connector; the italicized sentence of example (8) is connected to previous discourse by temporal linking; and the italicized sentence of (9) derives its coherence with previous discourse through the progressive aspect, which implies that the predicate's event is simultaneous with Andrew's thought act. All the sentences have in common the introduction of referents that are not mentioned within the preceding *local* discourse context (i.e. *Mr Parry*, *Edith*, and *the tide*). It is these abrupt topic shifts that distinguish passages like (2) and (7)–(9) from passages like (1), which derive their coherence from referential linking.

In comparing passages from Woolf to Gutwinski's claims about passages from James and Hemingway, we can conclude that Woolf's texts display a greater variety of cohesive devices than Hemingway's and James' do. (Recall that the vast majority of cohesive devices in the James and Hemingway passages analysed by Gutwinski were referential links.) Furthermore, the coherence of RST passages in Woolf's prose is often achieved by linguistic features that do not involve the *repetition* of referents, but rather involve the introduction of new referents into the local discourse context.

6.3.1 Spoken vs written discourse

The abrupt topic shifts displayed in passages such as (2) and (7)–(9) are similar to the sudden topic shifts of spoken discourse. Because spoken discourse is highly context-bound and often composed 'on the run', it is often characterized by sudden shifts in topic – these shifts being responses to ongoing events in the context of the speech event (Fillmore 1981). Fillmore provides the following hypothetical example of spoken discourse:

(10) [a] Yes, I've enjoyed living in California a great deal. [b] My, this soup is magnificent. [c] And in fact I can't imagine ever wanting to live anywhere else. [d] Oh my God, what's happening? [e] The whole house is moving.

(Fillmore 1981: 148)

Sentences [b] and [e] are like the italicized sentences in (7)–(9) to the extent that they introduce referents that have not been previously mentioned in the local discourse context. Passage (10) is coherent, of course, as spoken discourse by virtue of the fact that it is produced in a particular situation. That is, the sudden shifts in topic make sense as responses to events in the immediate environment of the speaker. I have argued that sentences such as the italicized ones of (7)–(9) are coherent with previous discourse, in part, as a result of their particular linguistic features (e.g. they have semantic connectors, they contain predicates with unanchored tenses or predicates in progressive aspect). While coherent with previous discourse, however, the italicized sentences of (7)–(9) reflect the fragmented nature of characters' inner perceptions precisely because of their sudden topic shifts. Just as the sudden topic shifts of (10) are interpreted as a speaker's response to events in the speech situation, so the topic shifts of (7)–(9) are interpreted as characters' responses to events in the narrative world. Thus, it is the nature of the linguistic phenomena of semantic connector linking, temporal linking, and the progressive aspect (as opposed to referential linking) that allows coherence to be imposed on passages such as (7)–(9) but at the same time creates an impression of 'incoherence' or spontaneity characteristic of the inner speech of characters. Texts that rely heavily on referential linking to achieve their formal connectedness (such as the Hemingway and James passages analysed by Gutwinski) do not display the superficial 'incoherence' emblematic of many of Woolf's passages.

6.3.2 Resolution vs revelation narratives

The analysis of literary narrative within structuralist theory has presupposed a distinction between 'story' (*histoire*), the sequence of actions or events of a narrative, and 'discourse' (*discours*), the means by which the events are ordered and presented. In discussing the 'story' component of narratives, Chatman (1978) distinguishes between two types of narrative: the traditional narrative of 'resolution' and the modern novel of 'revelation'. This distinction seems to be based on the type of linguistic material that constitutes the 'story'. The basic movement in the narrative of 'resolution' focuses on the question 'what will happen next?' Thus, the particular events as well as their particular sequence contribute significantly to the overall interpretation of the text.

In narratives of 'revelation', there is a sense that nothing changes. Chatman (1978: 48) states: 'It is not that events are resolved (happily or tragically) but rather that a state of affairs is revealed'. In fact, the particular events that do take place in the narrative of 'revelation' are often of little importance to the narrative as a whole. Whether

CONCLUSIONS

Clarissa Dalloway in *Mrs Dalloway* spends her time shopping or writing letters or daydreaming is not as crucial as what any one of these events will reveal about what is going through her mind, this being a crucial concern of the narrative of 'revelation'.

As novels of revelation, *To the Lighthouse* and *Mrs Dalloway* have as their major function the representation of the consciousness of characters. It is perhaps not surprising, then, that the linguistic means by which coherence is often achieved in these texts does not involve the repetition of referents. Rather, the texts are frequently characterized by sudden topic shifts, typical of unplanned, spoken discourse and the inner speech of characters.

7

IMPLICATIONS: THE FOREGROUND/ BACKGROUND DISTINCTION

7.0 INTRODUCTION

At least two kinds of questions concerning the foreground/background distinction arise from the analysis presented in this book. First, is it incorrect to equate narration with foreground material and RST with background material as Banfield does (see Chapter 1)? And if so, how should the foreground/background distinction be drawn in these texts? Second, are the linguistic correlates of foreground and background material in these texts comparable to those found in simpler texts?

7.1 THE FOREGROUND/BACKGROUND DISTINCTION

As stated in Chapter 1, Banfield (1982) seems to equate narration with foreground material and RST with background material to the extent that her definitions of narration are strikingly similar to definitions of foreground material that appear in the discourse analysis literature (Hopper 1979; Reinhart 1982). For example, she claims that the sentence of narration 'narrates events' and 'holds the essence of the narrative'. 'The events are set forth chronologically, as they occurred' (Banfield 1982: 164–5). In addition, Banfield associates the aorist/imparfait aspectual distinction in French and the simple past/past progressive distinction in English (at least, with some predicate types) with narration and RST, respectively. This particular aspectual distinction has been reported in the discourse analysis literature to correlate with foreground and background material in narrative discourse (Hopper 1979; Dry 1981, 1983; Chvany 1984).

IMPLICATIONS

One of the problems in evaluating Banfield's claims regarding the relationship between narration/RST and foreground/background is the difficulty in arriving at precise definitions of the terms, foreground and background. Hopper and Thompson (1980: 280), for example, claim that foreground material is material that 'supplies the main points of the discourse', while background material is 'that part of a discourse which does not immediately and crucially contribute to the speaker's goal'. Other treatments of foreground/background material, as discussed in Chapter 1, view the distinction somewhat differently (Hopper 1979; Reinhart 1984; Labov 1972). Reinhart, for example, defines the foreground as the part of a text that serves to move the narrative through time and the background as durative/descriptive material that does not advance the story-line of a narrative. She views the foreground/background distinction as analogous with the distinction made in gestalt theory between figure and ground. Just as the ground provides the background for a figure in a painting, so the background of a narrative text provides the context (description and elaboration) against which the temporal events of the narrative occur. Reinhart argues convincingly that the foreground/background distinction is better conceived in terms of temporal/non-temporal information rather than in terms of important/unimportant information. Certainly in literary narratives such as the ones under discussion here, it seems incorrect to say that non-plot-advancing linguistic material does not 'immediately and crucially contribute to the speaker's (writer's) goal' as there seems to be no principled way of determining, for instance, that descriptions of characters are less important to the overall effect of the texts than temporally ordered events.

While Hopper and Thompson (1980) and Reinhart (1984) differ in the way that they define the discourse function of foreground/background material, they do agree on just what linguistic material within texts constitutes the foreground vs the background. For Hopper and Thompson, foregrounded clauses correlate strongly with highly transitive clauses. Because a highly transitive clause is one that is punctual, perfective, and affirmative, foregrounded clauses (in Hopper and Thompson's terms) will also correlate with clauses that serve to move the narrative through time because the perception of time movement requires that an event be presented as complete (i.e. punctual and perfective). These, of course, are the clauses that Reinhart considers to be part of the foreground of a text. Given the difficulty in determining what constitutes the most important information of a discourse, I will assume, following Reinhart (1984), that in narrative discourse the foreground is linguistic material that charts the progress of a narrative through time whereas the background is durative and descriptive linguistic material. In the following passage, for example, the italicized sentences comprise the foreground of the discourse:

(1) *Mrs Morel looked down at him.* She had dreaded this baby like a catastrophe, because of her feeling for her husband. *And now she felt strangely towards the infant.* Her heart was heavy because of the child, almost as if it were unhealthy, or malformed. Yet it seemed quite well. . . .
  'He looks as if he was thinking about something – quite sorrowful,' said Mrs Kirk.
  Suddenly, looking at him, the heavy feeling at the mother's heart melted into passionate grief. She bowed over him, and a few tears shook swiftly out of her very heart. The baby lifted his fingers.
  'My lamb!' she cried softly.
  And at that moment she felt, in some far inner place of her soul, that she and her husband were guilty.
  The baby was looking up at her. It had blue eyes like her own but its look was heavy, steady, as if it had realized something that had stunned some point of its soul.
  (*Sons and Lovers*, 50)

Notice that several of the sentences in the initial paragraph constitute background material. They represent states that obtain both before and after the timeline events of the narrative (e.g. *Her heart was heavy because of the child, . . . Yet it seemed quite well*) or activities that occurred before the events on the main time axis of the narrative (e.g. *She had dreaded this baby like a catastrophe . . .*). Likewise, the final paragraph of the passage exhibits background material, events and states that are represented as simultaneous with the previously mentioned timeline event.

Recent work in discourse semantics (Dry 1983; Dowty 1986) has identified certain predicate-types in simple or perfective aspect as pushing the reference time of a narrative forward (i.e. predicates that constitute Reinhart's foreground). For Dry (1983), predicates that refer to the initial and/or final endpoints of situations create the impression of time movement. Because the simple past tense in English refers to the endpoints of the situation that its predicate represents (Smith 1983), sentences such as those in (2) below move the reference time of the narrative forward:

IMPLICATIONS

(2) Fred walked into the room. The janitor sat down on the couch.

On the other hand, the progressive refers to a point that is not an endpoint, and thus the second sentence of (3) below does not move time forward:

(3) Fred walked into the room. The janitor was sitting down on the couch.

This aspectual alternation between the simple past and past progressive interacts with predicate-type (what Smith, 1983, calls situation aspect) to the extent that only events (as opposed to states) in the simple past tense will create new reference points. Using Vendler's (1967) taxonomy of predicate-types, Dry categorizes both achievements and accomplishments as events and both activities and statives as states. Within this system, achievements are defined as situations with a punctual occurrence having a natural endpoint (i.e. reaching the top, blinking). Accomplishments also have natural endpoints but are situations of greater duration than achievements (i.e. building a house, typing a letter). Activities (i.e. running, swimming) and statives are classified as states rather than events because neither have natural endpoints, only arbitrary ones. Statives are different from activities in that no energy is required to maintain them (i.e. knowing someone, being short, owning a car).[1] The effect of predicate-type on the movement of narrative time is illustrated below:

(4) Fred walked into the room. Susan *got up* from her chair.

(5) Fred walked into the room. Susan *sat* in her chair.

Because the second sentence of (4) contains the achievement predicate, *got up*, it refers to the endpoint of this situation and therefore is interpreted as denoting an event that occurs later than the previous sentence's event. In contrast, the second sentence of (5) contains an activity predicate and thus the state denoted by this predicate is interpreted as overlapping with the previous sentence's event. Dry draws the following generalization on the basis of examples such as (2)–(5) above: main clause achievement and accomplishment predicates in simple aspect will serve to propel the reference time of a narrative forward.[2] In our terms, clauses with these linguistic properties will constitute the foreground of a narrative. Returning to passage (1), we see that the italicized sentences comprising the foreground do, indeed, display achievement and accomplishment predicates in simple aspect.[3]

7.2 NARRATION/RST AND FOREGROUND/BACKGROUND

Having established more precise definitions of foreground and background, we can now consider how this dichotomy is related to the narration/RST distinction. Recall that, in the texts under investigation here, narration refers to linguistic material presented from an objective viewpoint, that is, material that does not represent events or descriptions through the consciousness of any character. By contrast, RST refers to events and descriptions within the narrative that are conveyed through the consciousness of a character. One question that arises, then, is whether narration can be equated with foreground material, as Banfield suggests. Certainly, there are many passages in *To the Lighthouse* and *Mrs Dalloway* where achievement and accomplishment predicates in the simple past tense serve to move time forward in the narrative world and where the designated events are not relayed from any character's point of view. Consider the following example:

(6) She supposed it was all right leaving him to his own devices, Mrs Ramsay *said*, wondering whether it was any use sending down bulbs; did they plant them? 'Oh, he has his dissertation to write,' *said* Mr Ramsay. She knew all about *that* [emphasis Woolf's], *said* Mrs Ramsay. He talked of nothing else. It was about the influence of somebody upon something. 'Well, it's all he has to count on,' *said* Mr Ramsay. 'Pray Heaven he won't fall in love with Prue,' *said* Mrs Ramsay. He'd disinherit her if she married him, *said* Mr Ramsay.

(*To the Lighthouse*, 77)

While the semantic content of the root-Ss in the SCPs above is understood as reflecting Mr or Mrs Ramsay's point of view, the accomplishment predicates *said* of the SCPs' parentheticals report the speech acts from an objective point of view, i.e. from a vantage point that is equi-distant from all characters. In addition, because these accomplishment predicates are in simple aspect (the simple past tense), they move time forward in the narrative. The speech acts are interpreted as occurring consecutively in the narrative world, with each SCP's event understood as occurring later than the previous SCP's event.

IMPLICATIONS

While the linguistic material of narration can clearly create the impression of time movement (i.e. constitute the foreground), non-temporal material in these texts can also be conveyed from the narrator's objective point of view. The italicized material in the passage below, for example, is clearly durative and descriptive in nature (a description of Mr Ramsay), yet it is not relayed through the consciousness of a character:

(7) Had there been an axe handy, a poker, or any weapon that would have gashed a hole in his father's breast and killed him, there and then, James would have seized it. *Such were the extremes of emotion that Mr Ramsay excited in his children's breasts by his mere presence; standing, as now, lean as a knife, narrow as the blade of one, grinning sarcastically, not only with the pleasure of disillusioning his son and casting ridicule upon his wife*, who was ten thousand times better in every way than he was (James thought), *but also with some secret deceit at his own accuracy of judgement.*

(*To the Lighthouse*, 6)

Thus, it is incorrect to *equate* narration with the foreground, as both foreground and background material are included within the category of narration.

The question of whether RST should be equated with background material is a more difficult one to answer. Much RST material is similar to passage (1) of Chapter 6 (repeated here) in that a description of one character (Minta, in this example) is conveyed to the reader through the consciousness of another (Andrew, in this example).

(8) Minta, Andrew observed, was rather a good walker. She wore more sensible clothes than most women. She wore very short skirts and black knickerbockers. She would jump straight into a stream and flounder across. He liked her rashness, but he saw that it would not do – she would kill herself in some idiotic way one of these days. She seemed to be afraid of nothing – except bulls. At the mere sight of a bull in a field she would throw up her arms and fly screaming, which was the very thing to enrage a bull of course. But she did not mind owning up to it in the least; one must admit that. She knew she was an awful coward about bulls, she said. She thought she

must have been tossed in her perambulator when she was a baby. She didn't seem to mind what she said or did.

(*To the Lighthouse*, 86)

The question that arises is whether RST portions of these texts are always durative and descriptive in nature and, thus, part of the background. While descriptive impressions of characters are often relayed from the vantage point of another character in these texts (as in (8) above), it is also possible for *events* of the narrative present to be attributed to the consciousness of a character. The kind of sentence discussed in Chapter 5 and exemplified below illustrates this phenomenon.

(9) She [Mrs Ramsay] could see the words echoing as she spoke them rhythmically in Cam's mind, and *Cam was repeating after her* how it was like a mountain, a bird's nest, a garden and there were little antelopes, . . .

(*To the Lighthouse*, 132)

(10) Like all stupid people, he had a kind of modesty too, a consideration for what you were feeling, which, once in a way at least, she found attractive. Now *he was thinking*, not about himself or about Tolstoy, but *whether she was cold*, whether she felt a draught, whether she would like a pear.

(*To the Lighthouse*, 125)

(11) She [Mrs Ramsay] looked at him thinking to find this shown in his face; he [Mr Ramsay] would be looking magnificent. . . . But not in the least! *He was screwing his face up*, he was scowling and frowning, and flushing with anger.

(*To the Lighthouse*, 110)

(12) . . . for she [Cam] thought, looking at James who kept his eyes dispassionately on the sail, or glanced now and then for a second at the horizon, you're not exposed to it, to this pressure and division of feeling, this extraordinary temptation. *Her father was feeling in his pockets*; in another second, he would have found his book.

(*To the Lighthouse*, 192)

(13) Looking at his hand he [William Bankes] thought that if he had been alone dinner would have been almost over

IMPLICATIONS

now; he would have been free to work. Yes, he thought, it is a terrible waste of time. The children were dropping in still. *'I wish one of you would run up to Roger's room,' Mrs Ramsay was saying.*

(*To the Lighthouse*, 102)

The italicized sentences in the above passages all contain achievement or accomplishment predicates in the past progressive.[4] As argued in Chapter 5, the existence of the progressive aspect in these sentences facilitates their interpretation as narrative present events relayed through the consciousness of a character. For example, it is Mrs Ramsay who observes Mr Ramsay screwing up his face in (11), Cam who observes her father feeling in his pockets in (12), and William Bankes who observes Mrs Ramsay's speech act in (13). The question is whether these narrative present events constitute foreground or background material.

While the progressive aspect does not normally refer to the endpoints of situations, Dowty (1986) has claimed that progressives such as the ones in passages (9)–(13) allow a quasi-inceptive interpretation in that a character's perception of the progressive predicate's event begins upon the event's mention in the text. That is, the sentences convey a character's initial observation of an event that is already in progress. This claim is supported by the fact that a punctual adverbial (one that normally occurs with events that have endpoints) can be juxtaposed with such a progressive.

(14)   ... for she thought, looking at James who kept his eyes dispassionately on the sail, or glanced now and then for a second at the horizon, you're not exposed to it, to this pressure and division of feeling, this extraordinary temptation. *Her father was feeling in his pockets all of a sudden*; in another second, he would have found his book.

The adverbial, *all of a sudden*, is attributed to the daughter's perception in passage (14); in other words, the sudden movement is what she perceives, not necessarily what has just occurred in the depicted world. By contrast, the juxtaposition of the same adverbial with a progressive in the passage below yields somewhat deviant discourse.

(15)   The house was bought in 1970 and occupied without incident or disturbance until one night in December of

1981. Around sunset that night, the wind began to howl around the old house. The shutters were creaking and *all of a sudden were coming off their hinges*.
(based on passage from Aristar and Dry, 1982: 2)

Because the italicized sentence's event in (15) is not relayed from the perspective of a character (there is no predicate designating a character's communication or consciousness with which the italicized event is simultaneous), it is impossible to attribute the adverb of punctuality to a character's perceptions. The progressive, here, does not refer to the initial point of a character's observation of the event. Thus, the italicized sentence of (15) is odd within its context relative to the italicized sentence of (14) in its context.

The claim is that sentences like the italicized ones of (9)–(13) (i.e. the sentences that are the focus of Chapter 5) refer to the initial point of their predicate's event, from the perspective of a character. Recall that Dry has argued that the illusion of time movement in narrative discourse is triggered by predicates that refer to initial and/or final points of situations. Thus, it is normally achievements and accomplishments in simple aspect that create the impression of time moving forward. Because progressives such as the ones in (9)–(13) are unique in their quasi-inceptive interpretation, I suggest (following Dowty 1986) that they are also unique in their discourse function. They move time forward in the narrative world to the extent that, from the perspective of a character, a new reference time is introduced into the text. Such sentences, then, represent foreground information within RST. That is, just as descriptive and durative material (i.e. the background) can be conveyed through the consciousness of characters in these texts, so events that move the narrative through time can be relayed from the point of view of a character.

What seems clear from this discussion is the inadequacy of the simple binary distinction between foreground and background for describing texts conveyed from a multiplicity of perspectives. Reinhart (1984), employing a visual analogy, has suggested that complex narrative texts may contain 'layers' of foreground in the same way that a painting can show a figure resting on a figure resting on a figure. In texts with multiple points of view, the appropriate visual analogy would seem to be a Picasso painting in which a figure (or the foreground) is presented simultaneously from several viewpoints. The texts under investigation here are comparable to such paintings because they represent foreground and background material from different points of view: the objective viewpoint of the formal speaker of the text as opposed to the subjective viewpoints of characters. In the passage below, for example, Lily Briscoe's speech event is initially relayed from the objective perspective of the narrator (i.e. *she said*). The second mention of this same event (i.e. *She was saying*), however, relates the speech act from Mr Tansley's point of view.

(16)   'Oh, Mr Tansley,' *she said*, 'do take me to the Lighthouse with you. I should so love it.'
   She was telling lies, he could see. *She was saying* what she did not mean to annoy him, for some reason. She was laughing at him.

(*To the Lighthouse*, 99–100)

Not only, then, can these texts convey foreground and background material from various viewpoints, they can also, like the Picasso painting, present the same event or figure (i.e. foreground) from two points of view simultaneously.

7.3 LINGUISTIC CORRELATES OF FOREGROUND AND BACKGROUND MATERIAL

As stated above, Dry's generalization regarding predicates that move time forward in a narrative (what I am calling the foreground of a narrative) concerns aspect and predicate-type. Specifically, achievement and accomplishment predicates in simple aspect will create the impression of time movement within narrative discourse. In line with other work on the foreground/background distinction (Hopper 1979, 1982; Chvany 1980, 1984), Dry's generalization associates the perfective/imperfective aspectual alternation with foreground and background material, respectively (at least, where achievement and accomplishment predicates are concerned). What we have already seen in texts characterized by RST, however, is that the past progressive (imperfective aspect) does *not* always signal background information. Within RST discourse units, the past progressive can represent an event with an initial endpoint and, thus, can function to propel the reference time of a narrative forward. Similarly, these texts display instances of achievement and accomplishment predicates in the simple past (perfective aspect) that do *not* signal foreground information. Consider the examples below:

(17)   Minta, Andrew observed, was rather a good walker.

She wore more sensible clothes than most women. She wore very short skirts and black knickerbockers. . . . She seemed to be afraid of nothing – except bulls. At the mere sight of a bull in a field she would throw up her arms and fly screaming, which was the very thing to enrage a bull of course. But she did not mind owning up to it in the least; one must admit that. She knew she was an awful coward about bulls, she *said*. She *thought* she must have been tossed in her perambulator when she was a baby. She didn't seem to mind what she said or did.

(*To the Lighthouse*, 86)

(18) For always, he thought, there was something incongruous to be worked into the harmony of her face. She *clapped* a deer-stalker's hat on her head; she *ran* across the lawn in galoshes to snatch a child from mischief.

(*To the Lighthouse*, 35)

(19) They were both out of things, Mrs Ramsay had been thinking, both Lily and Charles Tansley. Both suffered from the glow of the other two. He, it was clear, felt himself utterly in the cold; no woman would look at him with Paul Rayley in the room. . . . With Lily it was different. She *faded* under Minta's glow; *became* more inconspicuous than ever, in her little grey dress with her little puckered face and her little Chinese eyes.

(*To the Lighthouse*, 119)

(20) When he felt like that he went to the Music Hall, said Dr Holmes. He *took* a day off with his wife and *played* golf.

(*Mrs Dalloway*, 100–1)

Notice that the italicized predicates are achievements or accomplishments in the simple past tense (perfective aspect).[5] While in other contexts the italicized predicates would have the effect of propelling the narrative through time, in (17)–(20) they represent habitual events or states as perceived through the consciousness of a character (i.e. a character's RST). Notice also that the sentences containing the italicized predicates above are all referentially linked to a preceding SCP. That is, they belong to the same RST unit as the preceding SCP. (The SCP, of course, indicates explicitly whose source consciousness orients surrounding discourse.) In extending an RST interpretation

IMPLICATIONS

beyond the domain of a single sentence, referential linking allows a parenthetical such as *Andrew observed* in (17) to have scope over more than one sentence. The referentially linked sentences are thus interpreted as 'complements' of their parentheticals, and their simple past tenses (with achievements and accomplishments) do not receive their 'usual' interpretation in independent sentences. That is, they do not function to propel the reference time of the narrative forward.

Throughout this book, I have argued that local discourse context is essential to explaining the point of view interpretation of independent sentences. Because local discourse context determines, in part, whether sentences are understood as RST or narration, it also determines, in part, whether the simple past tense/past progressive alternation will correlate with foreground and background material, respectively. Thus, by showing how discourse context is relevant to the interpretation of point of view, I have also demonstrated how local discourse context is relevant to the discourse function of the simple past/past progressive alternation in English. Whether a predicate in the simple past tense is understood as pushing a narrative through time or as a character's state or habitual event of RST (i.e. 'back-shifted' from its simple present tense form) is influenced by its relation to the surrounding context. (In (17)–(20), for example, the italicized predicates are in sentences that are referentially linked to SCPs and, hence, are part of RST discourse units.) And whether a predicate in the past progressive is understood as representing durative and descriptive material or the initial point in a character's perception of an event is also influenced by its relation to local discourse context. (In (9)–(13), for example, the events in past progressive are contemporaneous with predicates designating a character's communication or consciousness.) Thus, for complex narrative texts at least, we must conclude (following Comrie 1986) that the simple past and past progressive (perfective vs imperfective aspect) in English *assume* rather than signify specific discourse functions. Furthermore, the function a given aspectual form assumes is based, in part, on features of the local discourse context.[6]

NOTES

1 SENTENCE-BASED APPROACHES TO POINT OF VIEW

1 See Uspensky (1973) and Genette (1980) for theoretical treatments of point of view from a literary perspective.
2 Chatman (1978) claims that free, indirect style arose in nineteenth-century literature in most European languages. In French, this style is referred to as *'style indirect libre'* and in German as *'erlebte Rede.'*
3 Hooper and Thompson (1973) claim that root transformations, such as subject–auxiliary inversion, are grammatical in embedded sentences that are asserted. Hooper and Thompson's claims are discussed in more detail in Chapter 3.
4 While my approach to this issue differs from Banfield's, very little in my analysis hinges on this difference. That is, given Banfield's claim that sentences of these texts are 'speakerless', the question of how readers identify the point of view of sentences with no sentence-internal markers of RST still remains.
5 I assume, following Kuno (1987), that sentences of RST are ones in which the speaker (narrator) totally identifies with a character of the narrated events and that sentences of narration are ones in which the speaker remains equi-distant from all characters in reporting events or descriptions in the narrative world.
6 While Dry and Banfield may agree on the functional status of this type of linguistic material (i.e. that it is objective in its orientation), this is not to say that they agree on the question of whether these sentences have a speaker.
7 Labov's 'narrative clauses' do not imply objectivity in the same way that Banfield's sentences of narration do.

2 COHESION, COHERENCE, AND EPISODES

1 An exception to this is Blakemore (1988), who outlines an approach to coherence based on Sperber and Wilson's Principle of Relevance (1986). By this principle, hearers are said to process each new item of information

NOTES

on the assumption that speakers produce maximally relevant utterances for the minimum cost in processing. Linguistic expressions can function to constrain the relevance of the propositions they introduce. For example, in (i) below, Blakemore (1988: 247) explains that 'the relevance of the proposition introduced by *moreover* will be understood to lie in the fact that it is additional evidence for whatever conclusion is expected to be drawn from the first'.

  (i) John is a socialist. Moreover, he's a member of the Communist Party.

That is, a linguistic expression such as *moreover* will minimize a hearer's processing costs by specifying the nature of an utterance's relevance to on-going discourse. Thus, while Blakemore defines coherence independently of linguistic properties of discourse, linguistic expressions (e.g. cohesive devices) can be said to aid a hearer in computing the relevance of an utterance to other utterances within a discourse.

2 The Gricean-type implicature that arises from this lack of explicit coherence is that the student's academic abilities leave something to be desired. In Reinhart's terms, this inferencing process is an interpretive strategy used to impose coherence (implicit) on a discourse that is not explicitly coherent.

3 In Ehrlich (1988), I demonstrate that the mere occurrence of cohesive devices within second language learner discourse does not necessarily result in cohesive discourse. I formulate restrictions on referential and semantic connector linking to account for the deviance that results from the misuse of referential and semantic connector links.

4 Sentence topic has also been defined as the old or given information of a sentence (Chafe 1976). Reinhart (1982) points out that, in cases where a semantic sentence connector, and not referential linking, is responsible for the cohesion between two sentences (as in (ii) below), the topic of the second sentence will not necessarily be old or given information.

  (ii) The first man landed on the moon. At the very same moment, a young boy died in Alabama of untreated pneumonia.
                                                                    (Reinhart 1980: 176)

If the referential linking condition for cohesion is met, however, sentence topics will normally be old or given information.

5 The scene-setting expression of a sentence is the part of a sentence that specifies the spatial and temporal conditions of the event reported in the sentence.

6 The asterisk indicates pragmatic inappropriateness.

7 In cases where relative clauses (i.e. syntactic islands) do not contain presupposed information, they do allow a dominant reading. More specifically, sentences that function to introduce the head of a relative clause allow the content of their relative clauses to be interpreted as dominant, as demonstrated in (iii) below. Notice that the matrix verb here is somewhat reduced in terms of semantic content.

  (iii) Speaker: There are many people who have done that.

POINT OF VIEW

b. That's a lie, nobody has done that.

By the same token, non-island embedded clauses can be non-dominant with matrix verbs such as *lisp* or *editorialize* because such verbs have increased semantic content relative to a speech act verb such as *say*.

8 Violations of this restriction on referential linking are worse when the second NP is a pronominal. Chafe (1976) has explained the distinction between pronominal and nominal reference in terms of the difference between given and new information. Chafe (1976: 30) states that 'given (or old) information is that knowledge which the speaker assumes to be in the consciousness of the addressee at the time of the utterance. New information is what the speaker assumes he is introducing into the addressee's consciousness by what he says.' The primary linguistic consequence of this distinction, Chafe claims, is that given information will be expressed 'in a weaker and more attenuated manner than new information'. In English, this attenuation results in given information being weakly stressed and subject to pronominalization. Because the semantic content of a non-dominant clause does not constitute the main point of a speaker's utterance, this semantic content can be said not to be in the consciousness of the addressee (at least, relative to the semantic content of the utterance's dominant clause). Thus, pronominalizing an NP from a non-dominant clause would be treating new or 'non-activated' information as given or 'activated' information.

9 Within referential control, Reinhart (1980) includes what she calls direct control, indirect control, and implicit control. Direct control refers to cases where the topic or scene-setting expression of S2 is coreferential with previous expressions. Indirect control refers to cases where the topic is not itself coreferential with a previous expression, but contains a direct mention of a previously mentioned referent. And implicit control includes cases where the referent of the topic is a member of a class previously mentioned and cases where, in Halliday and Hasan's (1976: 286) terms, the topic has 'similar patterns of collocation' with a previously mentioned referent.

3 REFERENTIAL AND SEMANTIC CONNECTOR LINKING

1 I refer to the clause accompanying a parenthetical in a given SCP as the root-S of that SCP. I use this term because such clauses are characterized by main clause phenomena (i.e. root transformations), as will be demonstrated in the next section of this chapter.
2 For a discussion and refinement of Hooper and Thompson's semantic explanation regarding the distribution of root transformations, see Green (1976).
3 In examples (22) and (23), referential linking is achieved through the linking of sentence topics. As pointed out in Chapter 2, it is not essential that the topic of S2 be linked to a topic of S1 in order for the referential link condition of cohesion to be met. In the example below, referential linking occurs in (ia)–(ic) through the repetition of NPs that are sentence

NOTES

topics (i.e. *she*). Sentence (i)[d], however, takes as its topic the referent of a non-topic of the preceding sentence (the referent of *him*). Thus, while the NP of S1 participating in a referential link is always in a dominant clause of S1, it is not always the topic of S1. And notice that this type of referential linking (where the NP of S1 is a non-topic) serves to sustain an RST interpretation cross-sententially. The final two sentences of the passage are also understood as the perceptions of the referent of *he*.

(i) [a] She was telling lies, he could see. [b] She was saying what she did not mean to annoy him, for some reason. [c] She was laughing at him. [d] He was in his old flannel trousers. [e] He had not others.

(*To the Lighthouse*, 99)

4 I assume that referential linking is a transitive relation. That is, if sentence [b] is referentially linked to sentence [a], and sentence [c] is referentially linked to sentence [b], then sentence [c] is referentially linked to sentence [a]. In example (i) of the previous note, sentences [d] and [e] are not directly linked to sentence [a] (the only sentence in the passage that is explicitly marked as RST), but are linked by means of transitivity.

5 Banfield's use of the term 'stative' differs from the use of the term by Vendler (1967). Within Vendler's system of predicate-types, both activities and statives are classified as states because neither have natural endpoints. That is, every moment of an activity and stative is identical to every other moment. There is no natural endpoint to an activity, only an arbitrary one (i.e. running, swimming). Statives are different from activities in that no energy is required to maintain them (i.e. knowing someone, being tall, owning a house). Banfield seems to use the term 'stative' to refer to what Vendler calls 'state' (i.e. both activities and statives).

4 TEMPORAL LINKING

1 As noted in Chapter 1, Banfield (1982) argues that sentences of narration and RST in these texts are 'speakerless'. Thus, Banfield would undoubtedly disagree with Aristar and Dry's treatment of past time narratives whereby the RT of a narrative's main timeline events is anterior to the narrator's presumed *speech* time.

2 Notice that the corresponding sentence with an embedded-*that* clause, *Lily said that she disliked that sweet man immensely*, has a reading that is not semantically anomalous. This is the reading where the content of the complement clause is conveyed from the speaker's (as opposed to the parenthetical subject's) point of view.

3 The final sentence of (23) is also referentially linked to the preceding SCP. The combination of referential and temporal linking results in the sentence's unambiguous interpretation as the male character's RST.

4 The italicized sentence of (30) is more appropriate within its context than the italicized sentence of (29) is within its context. However, (30) is somewhat odd, especially in relation to (27). Notice that in (27) (Woolf's original passage), a paragraph boundary separates Lily Briscoe's RST from the evaluative prepositional phrase containing information incompatible

with Lily's knowledge. This segmentation creates an expectation on the part of the reader that a shift in topic or point of view will ensue.

5 It seems to be the case that the more links (referential, semantic connector, temporal) a sentence has with an explicitly marked sentence of RST, the more unambiguous its interpretation as RST is. It is possible that this linguistic difference (i.e. more as opposed to fewer links) correlates with Kuno's total vs partial identification of speakers with characters involved in narrative events.

6 While the second paragraph of (45) begins as narration, it later on becomes James's RST.

(i) And as if she had something she must share, yet could hardly leave her easel, so full her mind was of what she was thinking, of what she was seeing, Lily went past Mr Carmichael holding her brush to the edge of the lawn. Where was that boat now? Mr Ramsay? She wanted him.

Mr Ramsay had almost done reading. One hand hovered over the page as if to be in readiness to turn it the very instant he had finished it. He sat there bareheaded with the wind blowing his hair about, extraordinarily exposed to everything. He looked very old. He looked, James thought, getting his head now against the Lighthouse, now against the waste of waters running away into the open, like some old stone lying on the sand; he looked as if he had become physically what was always at the back of both of their minds – that loneliness which was for both of them the truth about things.

(*To the Lighthouse*, 230)

Hrushovski (1982) discusses the way that meaning is 'reconstructed' in texts vertically, resulting in retroactive interpretations. In the passage above, for example, when readers encounter *He looked, James thought, getting his head now against the Lighthouse* ..., they may retroactively identify the first half of this paragraph as James's RST. What is crucial about this passage, for my purposes, is that the second paragraph is *initially* identified as conveying a perspective (i.e. narration) that is distinct from the point of view conveyed in the preceding paragraph (i.e. Lily's RST).

5 ASPECT, COHERENCE, AND POINT OF VIEW

1 In (6), the interpretation of the italicized sentence as RST is facilitated by the NP *her father*. Kuno and Kaburaki (1975) and Kuno (1987) claim that this NP brings the viewing position of the sentence closer to the referent of her than to the speaker/narrator of the text. An NP such as *Mr Ramsay*, in the same context, would be more neutral in terms of point of view.

2 Passage (12) would be more acceptable if the simple past tense were transformed to the past perfect. In this case, the past perfect would represent an event anterior to the narrative present, conveyed from a character's point of view.

3 Within Vendler's (1967) classification of predicate-types, both achieve-

NOTES

ments and accomplishments are events with natural endpoints. They are distinguished from states (activities and statives), which do not have natural endpoints.

4 It is also possible for the progressive to describe events from a character's point of view if such events overlap with predicates denoting a character's perceptions. For example, in (i),

(i) Mary looked out of the window. Her father was feeling in his pockets.

the progressive aspect represents the event from Mary's point of view.

5 It is, of course, possible for a sentence in progressive aspect to be referentially linked to previous RST discourse. Consider the following example where the italicized sentence in progressive aspect is referentially linked to previous RST discourse.

(ii) Like all stupid people, he $_i$ had a kind of modesty too, a consideration for what you were feeling, which, once in a way at least, she found attractive. *Now he $_i$ was thinking, not about himself or about Tolstoy, but whether she was cold, whether she felt a draught.* . . .

(*To the Lighthouse*, 125)

6 CONCLUSIONS

1 Sentence [g] is referentially linked to sentence [f], which is temporally linked to a preceding SCP. Thus, sentence [g]'s interpretation as Mrs Ramsay's RST is facilitated by two linguistic features: the progressive aspect and referential linking.
2 A few of the sentences in passage (1) contain expressives (*of course* in [g] and *some song* in [l]) that contribute to the passage's interpretation as Andrew's RST. These are, of course, sentence-internal markers of RST.
3 We have seen that referential linking does not require topic to topic linking; the NP of S1 participating in a referential link only has to be contained within a dominant clause of S1 in order for cohesive discourse to result. The crucial distinction between passages like (1) and passages like (2) is that the former derive their cohesion from the repetition of referents whereas the latter do not. This means that passages like (1) are more likely to exhibit *gradual* topic shifts (if they have topic shifts at all) and passages like (2) are more likely to exhibit *abrupt* topic shifts.

7 IMPLICATIONS: THE FOREGROUND/ BACKGROUND DISTINCTION

1 Dowty (1986) points out that the predicate-type of English sentences is determined not by lexical main verbs alone, but rather by lexical main verbs in combination with other syntactic constituents of a sentence. Dowty (1986: 39) provides the following example of the way in which a prepositional phrase or noun phrase can convert an activity into an accomplishment.

(i) John walked. (activity)

(ii) John walked to the station. (accomplishment)
(iii) John walked a mile. (accomplishment)

2 Dry does point out exceptions to this generalization. First, certain adverbials indicate that a state has just come into being and, thus, sentences containing such adverbials will create the illusion of time movement. Second, Dry (1983: 45–6) says that 'subordinate clauses, reduced clauses, and participles can trigger a perception of temporal movement if they present the occurrence of a situation as new information and in *fabula* order and if they refer to a point on the timeline'.

3 The italicized sentence of the first paragraph in (1), *And now she felt strangely towards the infant*, does not have an accomplishment or achievement predicate-type. However, the presence of the adverbial, *now*, indicates that this activity has just begun. The initial point of the activity is referred to and, hence, the sentence creates the illusion of time movement.

4 In passage (9), I am assuming that the lexical main verb, *repeat*, in conjunction with the other constituents of its sentence, *after her how it was like a mountain, a bird's nest, a garden . . .*, is an accomplishment. If it is not interpreted in its iterative sense, notice its incompatibility (in simple aspect) with *for an hour*, an adverbial phrase that is only compatible with states and activities.

(iv) #Cam repeated the sentence once for an hour.

5 Dowty (1986) points out that some stative predicates are ambiguous between a stative and inceptive interpretation. With the latter interpretation, the predicates will trigger the perception of time movement as the initial point of the states is referred to. In passage (19), the predicate, *became more inconspicuous than ever*, receives an inceptive interpretation as indicated by its incompatibility with the durative adverbial, *for an hour*.

(v) #She became more inconspicuous than ever for an hour.

Thus, while not an achievement or accomplishment predicate, this stative does have the potential of moving the reference time of a narrative forward.

6 For further discussion of this point, see Ehrlich (1987 and forthcoming).

REFERENCES

Aristar, A. and Dry, H. (1982) 'The origin of backgrounding tenses in English', *Chicago Linguistic Society* 18: 1–13.
Auerbach, E. (1968) *Mimesis*, Princeton, NJ: Princeton University Press.
Banfield, A. (1973) 'Narrative style and the grammar of direct and indirect speech', *Foundations of Language* 10: 1–39.
Banfield, A. (1978) 'The formal coherence of represented speech and thought', *PTL: A Journal for Descriptive Poetics and Theory of Literature* 3: 289–314.
Banfield, A. (1981) 'Reflective and non-reflective consciousness in the language of fiction', *Poetics Today* 2: 61–76.
Banfield, A. (1982) *Unspeakable Sentences: Narration and Representation in the Language of Fiction*, London: Routledge & Kegan Paul.
Blakemore, D. (1988) 'The organization of discourse', in F. Newmeyer (ed.) *Linguistics: The Cambridge Survey*, 4, Cambridge: Cambridge University Press.
Brown, G. and Yule, G. (1983) *Discourse Analysis*, Cambridge: Cambridge University Press.
Chafe, W. (1976) 'Givenness, contrastiveness, definiteness, subjects, topics and point of view', in C. Li (ed.) *Subject and Topic*, New York: Academic Press.
Chatman, S. (1978) *Story and Discourse*, Ithaca, New York: Cornell University Press.
Chvany, C. (1980) 'The role of verbal tense and aspect in the narration of *The Tale of Igor's Campaign*', in A. Kodjak, M. Connolly, and K. Pomorska (eds) *The Structural Analysis of Narrative Texts*, Columbus, Ohio: Slavica Publishers.
Chvany, C. (1984) 'Foregrounding, transitivity, saliency in sequen-

tial and non-sequential prose', unpublished manuscript, MIT.
Comrie, B. (1976) *Aspect*, Cambridge: Cambridge University Press.
Comrie, B. (1986) 'Tense and time reference: From meaning to chronological structure of a text', *Journal of Literary Semantics* 15: 12–22.
Daneš, F. (1974) 'Functional sentence perspective in the organization of the text', in F. Daneš (ed.) *Papers on Functional Sentence Perspective*, Prague: Academia Publishing House of the Czechoslovak Academy of Sciences.
Dijk, T. van (1982) 'Episodes as units of discourse analysis', in D. Tannen (ed.) *Analyzing Discourse: Text and Talk*, Georgetown University Round Table on Languages and Linguistics, Washington, DC: Georgetown University Press.
Dijk, T. van and Kintsch, W. (1983) *Strategies of Discourse Comprehension*, New York: Academic Press.
Dillon, G. and Kirchhoff, F. (1976) 'On the form and function of FIS', *PTL: A Journal for Descriptive Poetics and Theory of Literature* 1: 431–40.
Dowty, D. (1986) 'The effects of aspectual class on the temporal structure of discourse: semantics or pragmatics?', *Linguistics and Philosophy* 9: 37–61.
Dry, H. (1975) 'Syntactic reflexes of point of view in Jane Austen's "Emma"', unpublished doctoral dissertation, University of Texas at Austin.
Dry, H. (1977) 'Syntax and point of view in Jane Austen's "Emma"', *Studies in Romanticism* 16: 87–99.
Dry, H. (1981) 'Sentence aspect and the movement of narrative time', *Text* 1: 233–40.
Dry, H. (1983) 'The movement of narrative time', *Journal of Literary Semantics* 12: 19–53.
Ehrlich, S. (1987) 'Aspect, foregrounding and point of view', *Text* 7: 363–76.
Ehrlich, S. (1988) 'Cohesive devices and discourse competence', *World Englishes* 7: 111–18.
Ehrlich, S. (forthcoming) 'Referential linking and the interpretation of tense', *Journal of Pragmatics* 14.
Emonds, J. (1976) *A Transformational Approach to English Syntax*, New York: Academic Press.
Erteschik-Shir, N. and Lappin, S. (1979) 'Dominance and the functional explanation of island phenomena', *Theoretical Linguis-*

REFERENCES

tics 6: 41–86.

Erteschik-Shir, N. and Lappin, S. (1983) 'Under stress: a functional explanation of English sentence stress', *Journal of Linguistics* 19: 419–53.

Fillmore, C. (1981) 'Pragmatics and the description of discourse', in P. Cole (ed.) *Radical Pragmatics*, New York: Academic Press.

Fox, B. (1987) *Discourse Structure and Anaphora*, Cambridge: Cambridge University Press.

Genette, G. (1980) *Narrative Discourse*, Ithaca, New York: Cornell University Press.

Giora, R. (1985) 'What's a coherent text', in E. Sozer (ed.) *Text Connexity, Text Coherence*, Hamburg: Helmut Buske Verlag.

Green, G. (1976) 'Main clause phenomena in subordinate clauses', *Language* 52: 382–97.

Grice, H.T. (1975) 'Logic and conversation', in P. Kohl and J. Morgan (eds) *Speech Acts*, Syntax and Semantics 3, New York: Academic Press.

Gutwinski, W. (1976) *Cohesion in Literary Texts*, The Hague: Mouton.

Halliday, M.A.K. and Hasan, R. (1976) *Cohesion in English*, London: Longman.

Hamburger, K. (1973) *The Logic of Literature*, Bloomington, Indiana: Indiana University Press.

Hinds, J. (1979) 'Organizational patterns in discourse', in T. Givon (ed.) *Discourse and Syntax*, Syntax and Semantics 12, New York: Academic Press.

Hooper, J. and Thompson, S. (1973) 'On the applicability of root transformations', *Linguistic Inquiry* 4: 465–97.

Hopper, P. (1979) 'Aspect and foregrounding in discourse', in T. Givon (ed.) *Discourse and Syntax*, Syntax and Semantics 12, New York: Academic Press.

Hopper, P. (1982) 'Aspect between discourse and grammar: An introductory essay for the volume', in P. Hopper (ed.) *Tense-Aspect: Between Semantics and Pragmatics*, Amsterdam/Philadelphia: John Benjamins.

Hopper, P. and Thompson, A. (1980) 'Transitivity in grammar and discourse', *Language* 56: 251–99.

Hrushovski, B. (1982) 'Integrational semantics: an understander's theory of meaning in context', in H. Byrnes (ed.) *Contemporary Perceptions of Language*, Georgetown University Round Table on

Language and Linguistics, Washington, DC: Georgetown University Press.
Jackendoff, R. (1972) *Semantic Interpretation in Generative Grammar*, Cambridge, Mass.: MIT Press.
Kuno, S. (1972) 'Functional sentence perspective', *Linguistic Inquiry* 3: 269–320.
Kuno, S. (1987) *Functional Syntax: Anaphora, Discourse and Empathy*, Chicago: University of Chicago Press.
Kuno, S. and Kaburaki, E. (1975) 'Empathy and syntax', in S. Kuno (ed.) *Harvard Studies in Syntax and Semantics*, Cambridge, Mass.: Harvard University Press.
Kuroda, S.-Y. (1973) 'Where epistemology, style and grammar meet: A case study from Japanese', in S. Anderson and P. Kiparsky (eds) *Festshrift for Morris Halle*, New York: Holt, Rinehart & Winston.
Labov, W. (1972) 'The transformation of experience in narrative syntax,' in *Language in the Inner City*, Philadelphia: University of Pennsylvania Press.
Leech, G. and Short, M. (1981) *Style in Fiction*, London: Longman.
Longacre, R. (1979) 'The paragraph as a grammatical unit', in T. Givon (ed.) *Discourse and Syntax*, Syntax and Semantics 12, New York: Academic Press.
Reichenbach, H. (1947) *Elements of Symbolic Logic*, New York: The Free Press.
Reinhart, T. (1980) 'Conditions for text coherence', *Poetics Today* 1: 161–80.
Reinhart, T. (1982) *Pragmatics and Linguistics: An Analysis of Sentence Topics*, Bloomington, Indiana: Indiana University Linguistics Club.
Reinhart, T. (1983) 'Point of view in language – the use of parentheticals', in G. Rauh (ed.) *Essays on Deixis*, Tubingen: Gunter Narr.
Reinhart, T. (1984) 'Principles of gestalt perception in the temporal organization of narrative texts', *Linguistics* 22: 779–809.
Rimmon-Kenan, S. (1983) *Narrative Fiction: Contemporary Poetics*, London: Methuen.
Ross, J.R. (1967) 'Constraints on variables in syntax', unpublished doctoral dissertation, MIT.
Smith, C.S. (1978) 'The syntax and interpretation of temporal expressions in English', *Linguistics and Philosophy* 2: 43–99.
Smith, C.S. (1980) 'Temporal structures in discourse', in H. Brekle, H. Heringer, C. Rohrer, H. Vater, and O. Werner *Time, Tense, and Quantifiers*, Tubingen: Max Niemeyer Verlag.

REFERENCES

Smith, C.S. (1981) 'Semantic and syntactic constraints on temporal interpretation', in P. Tedeschi and A. Zaenen (eds) *Tense and Aspect*, Syntax and Semantics 14, New York: Academic Press.

Smith, C.S. (1983) 'A theory of aspectual choice', *Language* 59: 479–501.

Sperber, D. and Wilson, D. (1986) *Relevance: Communication and Cognition*, Oxford: Basil Blackwell.

Stark, H. (1988) 'What do paragraph markings do?', *Discourse Processes* 11: 275–303.

Tamir, N. (1976) 'Personal narrative and its linguistic foundation', *PTL: A Journal for Descriptive Poetics and Theory of Literature* 1: 403–29.

Tomlin, R. (1987) 'Linguistic reflections of cognitive events', in R. Tomlin (ed.) *Coherence and Grounding in Discourse*, Amsterdam/Philadelphia: John Benjamins.

Uspensky, B. (1973) *A Poetics of Composition*, Berkeley, California: University of California Press.

Vendler, Z. (1967) *Linguistics in Philosophy*, Ithaca, New York: Cornell University Press.

LITERARY TEXTS

Lawrence, D.H. (1971) *Sons and Lovers*, Harmondsworth, Middlesex: Penguin Books. (First published 1913.)

Woolf, Virginia (1964) *Mrs Dalloway*, Harmondsworth, Middlesex: Penguin Books. (First published by The Hogarth Press 1925.)

Woolf, Virginia (1964) *To the Lighthouse*, Harmondsworth, Middlesex: Penguin Books. (First published by The Hogarth Press 1927.)

SUBJECT INDEX

accomplishment 87, 88–9, 109
achievement 87, 88–9, 109
activity 87, 109
Aktionsarten *see* aspect, situation
aorist 21, 26, 94, 106
aspect *see also* simple aspect, progressive aspect; situation 87, 109; viewpoint 87
assertion 42–5; *see also* dominance

background *see* foreground
back-shifted tenses 59–6, 78, 80, 94, 117; *see also* concordance of tense

camera angle 4; *see also* empathy
coherence 28–30, 95–9; semantic 27; conditions for 29, 30
cohesion 28, 29, 30–1, 95–9; *see also* referential linking, semantic connector linking, temporal linking
concordance of grammatical person 7–8
concordance of tense 6, 7–8, 13–14, 58, 59

deictics 21, 22–3, 65–7, 96–7
direct discourse, and indirect discourse 6–10; syntactic construct of 6–10, 16, 40
discourse units *see also* episode; demarcation of 56–7, 78–80, 99–101

dominance *see also* assertion; definition of 34; and lie-test 34–5, 45–6; and question-test 46–8; and syntactic islands 35–6

empathy 4–5
episode 27–8, 40, 99; *see also* discourse unit
event 87–8, 109; *see also* achievement, accomplishment
event time 61–2
expressive elements 9, 16, 17, 18–19, 20, 23–4

focus 33–4
foreground 1, and background 25–6, 106–17

imparfait 21, 94, 106; *see also* imperfective aspect
imperfective aspect *see* progressive aspect
impersonal discourse *see* personal and impersonal discourse
indirect discourse 7; *see also* direct discourse

left dislocation 32

macroproposition 27
modal 59–60

narrative, of resolution 104–5; of revelation 104–5; first person 6; third person 6; clause 1, 26

SUBJECT INDEX

paragraph *see also* discourse unit, episode boundaries 56–7, 78–80, 99
parenthetical, speaker-oriented 11–13; parenthetical-subject-oriented 11–14
parenthetical clauses 41, 45–8
past perfect tense 60, 77–8, 94
perfective aspect *see* simple aspect
personal and impersonal discourse 6–7, 10
phrase-structure rules 23
progressive aspect 21, 82, 83–5, 87–92, 93–4, 102–3, 106, 109–10, 115–17
pronominalization, forward 14; backward 13–14

reference time 61–2
referential linking 31–8, 95–7
reflexive pronoun 17–18
root, sentences 41; transformations 16, 42–5

scene-setting expression 33
semantic connector linking 38–9, 54–6, 97, 101–3

sentences containing parentheticals *see also* parenthetical, parenthetical-subject-oriented 41–56
sequence of tense *see* concordance of tense, back-shifted tenses
simple aspect 82, 83, 87–92, 106, 108–9, 115–17
simple past tense 21, 26, 60, 93–4 *see also* simple aspect
speech time 61–2
spoken discourse 103–4
state 87, 109; *see also* activity, stative
stative 22, 52, 87, 109
structure-preserving transformation 42

temporal linking 97, 101–3
tense *see* past perfect tense, simple past tense
topic, discourse 29, 56; shift 102–5; sentence 32–3
transitivity 107–8

AUTHOR INDEX

Aristar, A. 64, 114
Auerbach, E. 1

Banfield, H. 5, 10, 20–4, 25–6, 52–3, 106, 110
Brown, G. 28–9

Chatman, S. 104–5
Chvany, C. 26, 106, 115
Comrie, B. 87, 117

van Dijk, T. 27–8, 56, 100
Dillon, G. 10
Dowty, D. 114
Dry, H. 5, 17–20, 26, 64, 106, 109, 114, 115

Ehrlich, S. 34
Emonds, J. 42
Erteschik-Shir, N. 34–6, 43–6

Fillmore, C. 5, 24–5, 68–9, 103–4
Fox, B. 27, 100

Genette, G. 9
Giora, R. 28, 29
Grice, P. 28, 30
Gutwinski, W. 28, 59, 101, 103

Halliday, M.A.K. 28, 30–1, 59, 101
Hamburger, K. 10
Hasan, R. 28, 30–1, 59, 101
Hemingway, E. 101, 103

Hinds, J. 27
Hooper, J. 42–6
Hopper, P. 25, 26, 106, 107, 115
Jackendoff, R. 33
James, H. 101, 103

Kaburaki, E. 4
Kintsch, W. 27–8, 56
Kirchhoff, F. 10
Kuno, S. 4–5, 10, 20, 32
Kuroda, Y. 5, 10

Labov, W. 1, 26, 107
Lappin, S. 34–6
Leech, G. 10
Longacre, R. 27

Reichenbach, H. 61
Reinhart, T. 11–13, 25, 28, 29–31, 32–4, 38, 56, 59, 101, 106, 107–8, 114
Rimmon-Kenan, S. 10
Ross, J.R. 35

Short, M. 10
Smith, C. 60–4, 87, 109
Stark, H. 56

Tamir, N. 6, 10
Thompson, S. 42–6, 107
Tomlin, R. 27

Yule, G. 28–9